FONDUE,
CHAFING DISH and
CASSEROLE COOKERY

FONDUE, CHAFING DISH and CASSEROLE COOKERY

by Margaret Deeds Murphy

Drawings by Norman Pomerantz

A STUART L. DANIELS BOOK

Hawthorn Books, Inc.
Publishers   New York

To my husband,
my family and friends,
whose love and confidence
have sustained me in my career

CONTENTS

FOREWORD

Cooking is pleasure, frustration, sacrifice, boredom, elation, creativity, depression, fulfillment . . . all this and more. Those who brag about not being able to cook are missing a fascinating segment of life. Those of us who love to cook and approach the preparation of each recipe with joyful anticipation feel a bit sorry for those not so inclined.

My own love affair with cooking started when I was a little girl and my mother allowed me to experiment in the kitchen. My father was a most patient man who ate my concoctions with no complaints, which encouraged me to continue. It carried me through a course in home economics and into a varied and interesting career in the food field. Hopefully, the recipes presented here for use in the fondue pot, the chafing dish and the casserole will encourage those who are hesitant about cooking and will give new ideas and new approaches to those familiar with the art of preparing and serving food.

Margaret Deeds Murphy

INTRODUCTION

Fondue pots, chafing dishes and casseroles have a number of characteristics in common, which is the reason that recipes for their use were chosen to be presented in one volume.

For one thing, each of these pieces of equipment is high on the list of gifts given to new brides and each is frequently selected as a house or housewarming gift. Hundreds of thousands of fondue pots and chafing dishes are in the cupboards of as many households that are somewhat vague about the various uses to which they may be put. This, of course, is not true of the casserole, which has become a familiar item in many homes and shares with the other two the enhancement of convivial and informal entertainment.

The chafing dish has been with us for a long time, but recently there has been a rebirth of interest in its use. Fondue pots, in their present form, made a noticeable appearance only a short time ago. The proliferation and appeal of all three utensils stem from the growth of informal entertaining and, in our servantless times, the desire of the host and hostess to spend more time with their guests.

Foods prepared à la casserole are put in the oven just before the guests arrive and are brought forth to be served out of the same dish. With few exceptions a 10- to 20-minute delay in service doesn't affect their taste or quality. It makes for ease, relaxation and greater congeniality. Foods prepared and served from the fondue pot and chafing dish are cooked wholly or in part in front of the guests.

This book tells how you can get the most and best use out of these three utensils. If you don't own them now and are planning a purchase, these pages may guide you in your selection.

For the novice cook I have a few suggestions. Start with something simple. It is discouraging to have failures, and starting small is one way to avoid them. Even an experienced cook should hesitate to serve guests the result of the first trial of a recipe. I have been guilty of doing that occasionally over the years and have regretted it each time. So first try out the recipe on a close family member. Always read a recipe completely through before starting to cook. Better still, read it through while you still have time to shop for missing ingredients or equipment. After you have gained confidence in your ability, don't be afraid to experiment. Experimentation puts the mark of your own personality on recipes, which is a great part of the pleasure in cooking.

If you own all three pieces of equipment, it might be fun to plan a meal around them. For example:

Fondue Pot— Cucumber Soup (p. 33)
                      Assorted crackers
Casserole— Beef Chianti (p. 143)
                      Garlic bread
                      Salad of mixed greens, oil and
                          vinegar dressing
Chafing Dish—Cherries Jubilee (p. 118)
                      Demitasse

While this is a fairly extensive menu as far as our present day's informal entertaining goes, it still enables the host and/or hostess to spend a maximum amount of time with the guests. To make the service easy, use this plan: Serve the soup in the living room. Have the fondue pot, other utensils and ingredients on a tray, which is brought into the living room. Serve the main-course casserole, salad and bread either as a buffet in the same place or at table. Then the dessert and coffee can be brought into the living room and the cherries jubilee prepared in front of the guests, as indicated in the recipe.

I hope you have as much pleasure in the use of this book as I have had in its preparation. Enhance your enjoyment of life by using your fondue pot, chafing dish and casserole with love and imagination.

1.
FONDUES

A fondue pot is one of the few communal eating containers still in use in the Western world. The Swiss originated the fondue, not by design but out of necessity. In early times in Switzerland cheese and bread were made in the summer and fall to last all through the winter. Both became very hard, the bread so wooden that it literally had to be chopped with an axe. The cheese had to be heated over a fire to soften it and make it edible. Some long-forgotten innovator discovered that by melting the cheese in wine a delicious mix was made in which to dunk the bread and soften it. In the long, cold Swiss winters it was desirable to huddle round a fire and one large pot of cheese served for all. Each hungry peasant would dip his share of bread in the communal pot. Thus was Swiss Fondue born.

The custom continues to this day. When the necessity for using months-old bread was past, the fondue continued as a perfect dish to eat before the fire—after skiing or on any other appropriate occasion. As with many popular customs, this one soon spread beyond the national boundaries of its creators. And today, in the United States and other parts of the world, people are sitting around a communal fondue pot dunking pieces of bread in a delicious mixture of cheese and wine, flavored with kirsch and nutmeg.

However, those who think of the fondue only as a mixture of cheese, dry white wine and kirsch will be surprised to learn that there are a number of different kinds of fondue. The next most familiar fondue is probably the Fondue Bourguignonne, which consists of pieces of beef cooked in boiling oil. But more about that later.

Actually the word "fondue" causes quite a bit of confusion. It is derived from the French *fondre*—"to melt." A whole variety of dishes called fondues are in no respect related to the kinds of fondue we are discussing here—those made in a fonduc pot. Some softencd (mcltcd) vegetable dishes are called fondues, as are concoctions of butter, eggs, cream and breadcrumbs, which are baked in an oven; there are also baked desserts of chocolate, lemon or fruit.

The fondue recipes in this book fit the fondue pot, and those given should be cooked in that piece of equipment. In addition to the classical fondues, a number of variations are included, as well as various other recipes that extend the use of your fondue pot.

Fondues are versatile enough to serve as an hors d'oeuvre or as a main dish, as a late-supper meal or a festive Sunday brunch. The communal-pot atmosphere prevails and the host or hostess who likes to put on a show can cook a fondue with all the flourishes in front of the guests. The major characteristic of the fondue dishes with which we are concerned is that a group of people from four to eight in number can gather round a table, and each can dip a fork into the pot.

Fondue Pots

Because the use of the fondue pot has been expanded, it is being designed in ever-increasing variations in style and material. Many of the fondue vessels made for the Swiss

Fondue are more shallow and with wide-open tops, which is closer to the original. However, the narrower-topped versions help in the dunking operation.

There are small pots with only candle warmers for the heat source, which are designed for the Chocolate Fondue. No cooking is involved here. Enough heat is needed to keep warm the chocolate sauce into which fruit is dipped. A small quantity of the rich sauce will serve many people.

It is not necessary to have an assortment of these pots. While a ceramic open pot is generally recommended for the Swiss Fondue and a metal pot for the Fondue Bourguignonne, a good all-purpose metal pot of 1½ to 2 quarts will do for the cheese, the beef and even the chocolate fondues, as well as for the others. Preferably it should be enameled on the inside or be lined with a nonstick substance. A ceramic pot is not suitable for the Fondue Bourguignonne, since the oil must be boiled, and this might crack the pot. So, if you plan only one purchase, stick to the all-purpose pot.

A necessary accessory is a set of long-handled, two-pronged fondue forks, which are used to dip in the pot. Special plates that are sectioned for the sauces used in the Fondue Bourguignonne are also available but are not essential.

The Heat Source

The heat source can be an alcohol burner, canned fuel such as Sterno, or a butane-gas burner. Of the three, the butane-gas burner most nearly resembles a top range cooking unit. One on the market comes with its own handsome black iron trivet. Candle warming units are suitable only for keeping small quantities of precooked foods warm.

In cooking with a fondue pot there should be some way of regulating the heat. Butane-gas heaters, regulated by a dial or lever, offer the highest heat and the most efficient control. The alcohol burners and the canned fuel have a medium range of heat. The alcohol burners have either a series of air holes, which can be adjusted, or a lid, which can be moved over the top. Canned fuel generally has a lid that swings to open or close to adjust the amount of heat released.

Before attempting to make a fondue in front of guests, make certain that the heat source is strong enough to carry the entire operation through to the end. If not it may be best to prepare the initial phases in the kitchen, such as bringing the oil to boil for the Fondue Bourguignonne.

In using an earthenware or ceramic pot, one should be cautious as to the amount of heat that is exposed to the bottom of the pot. The heat should be kept low and should not be put in direct contact with the vessel.

CLASSIC FONDUE DISHES AND SOME VARIATIONS

Swiss Cheese Fondue

The fondue, which is known as the national dish of Switzerland, is a simple cheese mixture eaten directly from the pot by each diner dipping bite-size pieces of Italian or French bread speared to the end of a fork into the hot mixture. Because the cheese is so important, these notes on buying may help.

The original Swiss Fondue is made predominantly from what we call Swiss cheese but which is actually Emmenthaler (*Emmentaler,* after the Emme valley in the Bern canton, where it originated). Due to the popular use of the name "Swiss cheese," the average American store would not know what you wanted if you asked for Emmenthaler. Gruyere (after the Gruyere valley in Fribourg), the other popular Swiss-originated cheese, has retained its own name and can be purchased as such.

The imported Swiss cheese is a firm, smooth cheese with large round eyes (holes), a pale yellow color, and a sweet nutlike flavor. The rind of imported Swiss cheese (which is discarded in cooking) is marked "Switzerland Swiss Cheese."

Swiss cheese has become widely known because of the excellent American-produced variety. This domestic product is patterned after Emmenthaler.

7

Gruyere and Swiss Emmanthaler are "kissing cousins." Gruyere is less creamy and more salty and has smaller and more regular eyes. American Gruyere is also available.

Both are also sold as processed Swiss and Gruyere, but in buying cheese for fondue, be particularly careful to get the natural cheese. It has a more distinctive flavor and will give the characteristic texture to the fondue. Pasteurized processed cheese carries this information on the label.

Natural Swiss cheese is found in almost every grocery store that carries cheese. Natural Gruyere may be harder to locate. If you live near a cheese store you should be able to purchase both.

SWISS CHEESE FONDUE

ASSEMBLE INGREDIENTS:

1 clove garlic, cut in half
2 cups dry white wine (Rhine, Cortese, Riesling, Chablis, Neuchâtel)
1 tablespoon lemon juice
1 pound natural Swiss cheese, shredded or finely cut
3 tablespoons flour
3 tablespoons kirsch *
Nutmeg, freshly ground pepper or paprika to taste
2 loaves crusty Italian or French bread cut in cubes, crust on each cube

To cook the fondue in front of guests, the following prior behind-the-scenes work is necessary. Have the shredded or finely cut Swiss cheese (Emmenthaler) ready in a bowl. Near it should be the flour measured into an attractive small container and a clove of peeled garlic cut in half. In a cooking

* Or cognac if kirsch is not available.

performance one does nothing so prosaic as measuring ingredients before guests. Therefore one must practice privately to see how much wine to gurgle from the bottle to make approximately two cups. Decant two cups into a measure in the privacy of your kitchen. By estimating the amount left in the bottle you'll know how much to pour. The juice of half a fresh lemon will equal the amount needed for the recipe that follows, and again, it is part of the drama to squeeze the lemon juice directly from the lemon half. Wrap the lemon in cheesecloth to prevent the pits from dropping in the pot. If one isn't available, measure some bottled juice into a small container. Kirsch should be ready to pour, and whichever spices you prefer to add. You'll need a wooden spoon or fork for stirring, and don't forget to have the bite-size pieces of bread arranged neatly on a colorful napkin in a wicker basket. All these things can be prearranged on a tray ready for the performance ahead.

AT SERVING TIME:

Rub fondue pot with cut side of garlic. Discard. Pour in wine. Set over moderate heat. When wine is hot but not boiling, add lemon juice. Then dredge cheese lightly with flour and add by spoonfuls to the hot wine, stirring constantly with a wooden fork or spoon. Keep stirring until cheese is melted. Then add kirsch (or cognac) and spices, stirring until blended.

Serve and keep hot over burner. Each person in turn spears a bread cube through soft side into crust, dunks and swirls in fondue.

Makes 4 servings.

The crust that remains at the bottom of the fondue pot should be removed with a knife and divided among the diners. Many consider this the best part.

VARIATIONS:

1. *Fondue Gruyere:* Use Gruyere cheese instead of Swiss cheese in the same amount.
2. *Fondue Half-and-Half:* Use ½ pound of natural cheese and ½ pound of natural Gruyere cheese.
3. *Fondue Vermouth:* Substitute dry vermouth for the dry white wine.

Fondue Menu

When Swiss fondue is served as the main course the fondue pot is generally set in the center of the table so that the guests can help themselves. The table is set with plates and essential silverware. Cold, dry white wine or chilled apple juice makes a good accompaniment to the fondue. Serve a crisp cold salad of lettuce, watercress and grapefruit sections with French dressing. If you feel the need for a vegetable, buttered whole green beans would be a good choice.

For dessert, serve blueberry cake with ice cream and coffee.

Originally Swiss but now a universal fondue custom—if the lady loses her bread cube in the fondue, she pays with a kiss to the nearest man. If a man loses his bread, he provides the next round of drinks. But no tricking someone into losing his bread.

EGG-CHEESE FONDUE

ASSEMBLE INGREDIENTS:
   9 large eggs
   6 ounces natural Gruyere cheese (or Emmenthaler)
        grated (¾ cup)
   3 tablespoons butter
   ¼ teaspoon salt
   ¼ teaspoon freshly ground pepper (less if you like)
   2 loaves crusty Italian or French bread cut in cubes,
        with some crust on each cube

IN ADVANCE:
   Beat the eggs in a flat pan until the whites and yolks are well mixed.

AT SERVING TIME:
   Add cheese, butter, salt and pepper to eggs. Put mixture into fondue pot. Place on trivet over low heat and cook and stir until mixture begins to set but is still soft. Eat by spearing bread pieces on fork and dipping into cooked eggs and cheese mixture.

   Makes 4 servings.

If this fondue is to be served as a main course at a brunch, serve first a fruit salad made of chilled fresh pineapple, orange sections and Ribier grapes dressed with lemon, oil and paprika dressing. A rosé wine would be a good accompaniment, and for dessert Irish coffee.

FONDUE ITALIAN

ASSEMBLE INGREDIENTS:
>   1 pound natural mozzarella cheese or imported fontina
>   cheese
>   2 tablespoons flour
>   ½ pound fresh ricotta cheese
>   ¼ cup butter
>   ½ cup dry white wine
>   Freshly ground pepper
>   1 loaf French or Italian bread cut in cubes with a piece
>   of crust on each cube

IN ADVANCE:

Cut mozzarella or fontina cheese into small cubes and sprinkle with flour.

AT SERVING TIME:

Melt butter in fondue pot over moderate heat. Add cheeses and cook and stir until cheese begins to melt. Stir in wine and continue to stir until cheese is fully melted and wine blended into mixture. Season to taste with pepper. Reduce heat to low. To serve, spear bread cubes on fork and dip into fondue.

Makes 4 servings.

TIPS: When purchasing the cheese for this fondue, be sure *not* to get processed mozzarella. Processed cheese is always so labeled. Fondue Italian goes well with romaine and Belgian endive salad and black olives, and for dessert sliced peaches (fresh or frozen) and macaroons. Serve a robust red wine, such as Chianti, if desired.

Fondue Bourguignonne

The Fondue Bourguignonne, according to the legend, originated centuries ago in Burgundy's famous vineyards. Here, when the grapes are ripe to perfection, they must be picked immediately without stopping even for a midday meal. Some hungry soul had the idea of boiling a pot of oil to dunk-cook pieces of meat in spare moments so that he could eat on the run and neither his stomach nor the grapes would suffer. The idea caught on. Each picker brought his own meat, cooking to his own taste when he found time, and beef fondue was born. The fondue-loving Swiss developed the idea to its present form and credited the Burgundian grape-pickers by calling it Fondue Bourguignonne. This, too, may be regarded as a classic among fondues.

Cooking oil is heated in the fondue pot. In this oil each diner holds a small square of steak speared on a fork until cooked to the desired doneness. Two forks are needed, one for cooking and the other for eating, since the cooking fork gets very hot. The cooked steak is then dipped in any one or all of a variety of sauces that accompany the dish. There are special plates made for Fondue Bourguignonne that have several compartments on one side where the sauces may be placed. A number of sauces are suggested, and recipes for them follow the fondue recipe. Seasoned salt and pepper should also be placed within reach.

If there are more than four persons in the party, you may

want to have two fondue pots with hot oil so that the guests won't have to wait too long between their turns at cooking. The oil should be heated to 350° F. One can check this temperature, as it is reached when a bread cube browns in one minute. Meat cubes should be rare in 30 seconds, medium in 1 minute and well done in 1½ to 2 minutes.

FONDUE BOURGUIGNONNE

ASSEMBLE INGREDIENTS:

2 pounds beef tenderloin or good-quality boneless sirloin
3 to 4 cups cooking oil (amount depends on size of pot —it should be ½ to ⅔ full)*
An assortment of sauces, at least three
Seasoned salt
Seasoned pepper

IN ADVANCE:

Trim beef to remove all fat and any connective tissue. Cut into 1-inch cubes. Place cubes of beef on several platters so that meat will be easily accessible to all guests. Cover and store in refrigerator until cooking time. Prepare sauces and also store in refrigerator.

AT SERVING TIME:

Heat oil in fondue pot until bubbling. Each diner spears a cube of beef on a fork and holds it in the hot oil until it is done to the desired state. After transferring to a cool fork, the cooked beef is then dipped in any one of the sauces and eaten.

Makes 4 servings.

* The cooking oil may be half corn, vegetable or peanut oil mixed with half butter that has been clarified.

Sauces for Beef Bourguignonne

CURRY SAUCE

ASSEMBLE INGREDIENTS:

    ½ cup chopped onion
    ½ cup chopped celery
    2 tablespoons butter
    1 tablespoon chopped parsley
    ¼ teaspoon thyme
    Half a bay leaf
    ⅛ teaspoon ginger
    2 tablespoons flour
    1 teaspoon curry powder (or to your taste)
    2 cups light stock or bouillon

IN ADVANCE:

Sauté onion and celery in butter until tender. Stir in parsley, thyme, bay leaf, ginger, flour and curry powder. Add stock, stirring constantly and cook until mixture thickens. Continue cooking over low heat for 5 minutes. Strain. If made in advance, should be reheated and served hot.

Makes 2 cups.

SAUCE DIABLE

ASSEMBLE INGREDIENTS:
   ¾ cup dry white wine
   1 tablespoon vinegar
   1 tablespoon chopped shallots
   ¼ teaspoon thyme
   ¼ bay leaf
   Freshly ground pepper to taste
   1½ cups beef stock
   1 teaspoon beef extract
   2 tablespoons butter
   2 tablespoons flour

IN ADVANCE:
   Mix wine with vinegar, shallots, thyme, bay leaf and pepper in a small saucepan. Boil until reduced ⅓ the original amount. Add beef stock and beef extract. Cream butter and flour together and stir into liquid. Cook until mixture is thickened. Strain. Serve hot.

Makes 1¾ cups.

SOUR CREAM HORSERADISH SAUCE

ASSEMBLE INGREDIENTS:
   1½ cups dairy sour cream
   ¼ cup grated horseradish
   ½ teaspoon paprika

IN ADVANCE:
   Mix all ingredients together lightly. Chill well. Serve cold.

Makes 1½ cups.

CREAMED CURRY SAUCE

ASSEMBLE INGREDIENTS:
- ½ cup mayonnaise
- ½ cup sour cream
- 1 teaspoon lemon juice
- 1 teaspoon curry powder (or to taste)

IN ADVANCE:

Combine mayonnaise and sour cream. Add lemon juice and curry powder and blend until smooth. Serve cold.

Makes 1 cup.

SWEET PEPPER SAUCE

ASSEMBLE INGREDIENTS:
- 1 cup mayonnaise
- ½ cup sweet pepper relish
- 1 tablespoon chili sauce

IN ADVANCE:

Drain liquid from sweet pepper relish and discard. Mix relish with other ingredients. Serve cold.

Makes 1½ cups.

MUSTARD MAYONNAISE

ASSEMBLE INGREDIENTS:
- 1 cup mayonnaise
- 1 tablespoon prepared mustard (not English)

IN ADVANCE:

Mix ingredients until blended. Serve cold.

Makes about 1 cup.

ANCHOVY MAYONNAISE

ASSEMBLE INGREDIENTS:

3 flat anchovies
1 teaspoon capers
1 clove garlic, minced
1 teaspoon parsley, chopped
½ teaspoon dry mustard
1 cup mayonnaise

IN ADVANCE:

Mince anchovies and mix thoroughly with other ingredients.

Makes 1¼ cups.

AIOLI SAUCE

ASSEMBLE INGREDIENTS:

1 cup olive oil
1 tablespoon lemon juice
½ teaspoon salt
⅛ teaspoon freshly ground pepper
3 cloves garlic, peeled
2 egg yolks

IN ADVANCE:

Put about ⅓ cup of olive oil in blender container. Add lemon juice, salt, pepper and garlic. Cover and blend about 10 seconds. Add eggs, cover and blend 5 seconds longer. Remove cover and gradually pour remaining oil into center of blender. Stop blending when all oil has been used. Serve cold.

Makes about 1¼ cups.

WESTERN SAUCE

ASSEMBLE INGREDIENTS:
1 tablespoon butter
1 medium onion, minced
1 clove garlic, minced
1 8-ounce can tomato sauce
1 5-ounce can tomato paste
1 tablespoon Worcestershire sauce
Dash of Tabasco
1 tablespoon brown sugar
1 cup water

IN ADVANCE:
Heat butter in pan, sauté onion until transparent. Add tomato sauce and tomato paste. Stir and heat until just boiling. Add other ingredients and water and simmer until the consistency of sauce is what you desire.

Makes approximately 2 cups.

APPLE MUSTARD CREAM SAUCE

ASSEMBLE INGREDIENTS:
½ cup heavy cream
¼ cup canned apple sauce, chilled
1 tablespoon prepared mustard
⅛ teaspoon salt

IN ADVANCE:
Whip the cream until stiff. Fold in apple sauce, mustard and salt. Serve very cold.

Makes about 1 cup.

TARTAR SAUCE

ASSEMBLE INGREDIENTS:
- ½ cup mayonnaise
- ½ cup sour cream
- 2 scallions, finely chopped
- 2 tablespoons chopped dill pickle
- ¼ cup chopped, stuffed olives
- ¼ teaspoon salt
- ¼ teaspoon paprika

IN ADVANCE:

Mix all ingredients gently together and chill well.

Makes 1 cup.

HERBED TOMATO SAUCE

ASSEMBLE INGREDIENTS:
- 1 tablespoon butter
- 1 medium onion, chopped
- 1 can (8 ounces) tomato sauce
- 1 tablespoon vinegar
- 1 tablespoon lemon juice
- 2 tablespoons brown sugar
- 1 teaspoon salt
- 1 teaspoon dry mustard
- 1 bay leaf
- 1 clove garlic
- ⅛ teaspoon oregano
- ⅛ teaspoon basil
- ⅛ teaspoon thyme

IN ADVANCE:

Heat butter in small saucepan and sauté chopped onion until tender but not brown. Add remaining ingredients and simmer uncovered 15 minutes, stirring occasionally. Strain through sieve. Serve hot or cold.

Makes 1 cup.

HORSERADISH BROWN SAUCE

ASSEMBLE INGREDIENTS:

¼ cup butter
1 small onion, sliced
1 small carrot, peeled and sliced
½ bay leaf
4 whole cloves
4 tablespoons flour
½ teaspoon dry mustard
2 cups beef broth
4 tablespoons horseradish
Salt and freshly ground pepper to taste

IN ADVANCE:

Heat butter in skillet. Add onion, carrot, bay leaf and cloves. Cook until browned. Add flour and cook until browned. Remove from heat. Stir in mustard and then gradually add beef broth. Return to heat and cook and stir until mixture is thickened. Strain. Stir in horseradish. Season to taste with salt and pepper. Serve hot.

Makes about 2 cups.

BÉARNAISE SAUCE

ASSEMBLE INGREDIENTS:

¼ cup tarragon vinegar

⅓ cup dry white wine

2 shallots, chopped

1 sprig fresh tarragon*

4 peppercorns, crushed

4 egg yolks

½ tablespoon cream

½ cup melted, clarified butter

Salt and freshly ground pepper to taste

1 tablespoon chopped fresh tarragon*

IN ADVANCE:

Combine vinegar, wine, shallots, tarragon and pepper-corns in a small saucepan and cook until reduced one-half. Strain into a small glass bowl. Beat in egg yolks and cream. Set bowl over hot, not boiling, water and with a whisk gradually beat in butter. Continue to beat until sauce is thickened. Season to taste with salt and pepper. Fold in chopped fresh tarragon. Generally, Béarnaise sauce should be served directly after preparation.

Makes about 1 cup.

---

* Although fresh tarragon is preferable, ¼ teaspoon dried tarragon may be substituted for the sprig of fresh tarragon, and the same amount for the chopped fresh tarragon, if fresh tarragon is not available.

BÉARNAISE SAUCE NO. 2

ASSEMBLE INGREDIENTS:

2 shallots, chopped

½ cup butter

4 egg yolks

2 tablespoons tarragon vinegar

¼ teaspoon salt

Freshly ground pepper to taste

1 tablespoon chopped fresh tarragon*

1 tablespoon chopped fresh parsley

IN ADVANCE:

Cook shallots in butter until tender. Put shallots and butter into glass bowl and set over hot, not boiling, water. Using a whisk, beat in egg yolks one at a time. Continue cooking, stirring until mixture is thickened. Fold in remaining ingredients.

Makes about 1 cup.

SAUCE OLYMPIAD

ASSEMBLE INGREDIENTS:

4 tablespoons butter

3 tablespoons minced shallots

½ cup minced onion

2 cloves garlic, minced

⅓ cup cognac

1½ cups white wine

2 tablespoons tomato paste

1 tablespoon chopped parsley

1 tablespoon chopped fresh tarragon

Salt and freshly ground pepper to taste

* ¼ teaspoon dried tarragon leaves may be substituted for the chopped fresh tarragon.

IN ADVANCE:

Heat butter in small saucepan. Add shallots, onion and garlic and cook until tender but not browned. Add cognac and simmer until reduced one-half. Add remaining ingredients except salt and pepper and simmer until sauce is reduced one-third. Season to taste with salt and pepper. Serve hot.

Makes 1 cup.

COLD TOMATO MAYONNAISE

ASSEMBLE INGREDIENTS:

1 tablespoon chili sauce
½ teaspoon Worcestershire sauce
1 tomato, peeled, seeded and finely chopped
2 tablespoons chopped chives
1 tablespoon chopped parsley
1 cup mayonnaise

IN ADVANCE:

Gently mix chili sauce, Worcestershire sauce, tomato, chives and parsley into mayonnaise. Chill.

Makes 1½ cups.

HOT MUSTARD

ASSEMBLE INGREDIENTS:

1 cup dry mustard
1 teaspoon salt
2 teaspoons sugar
2 tablespoons hot water
¼ cup cider vinegar
2 teaspoons salad oil
2 teaspoons horseradish

IN ADVANCE:

Combine mustard with salt, sugar and hot water. Gradually blend in remaining ingredients.

Makes about ⅔ cup.

Other Sauces

In addition to these suggested sauces you may use any other homemade or commercially prepared sauces that appeal to your taste. These might include commercially prepared and bottled sauces, such as chili sauce, horseradish, Chinese sweet and sour duck sauce, tartar sauce, barbecue sauce, thick meat sauce, chopped chives, chopped piccalilli, your favorite mustard, or various chutneys, such as Major Grey's, and soy sauce.

Fondue Orientale

The third classic fondue from Switzerland is the Fondue Orientale. Many years ago a Swiss who was traveling in China was served a dish called Chrysanthemum Pot. Because the basic idea of diner-dunking in this dish was so similar to the Swiss Fondue principle, he told a noted chef about it when he returned home. The chef put it on his restaurant menu as Fondue Chinoise. It was discovered there a dozen years ago by a New York restaurateur, who perfected his own version and renamed it Fondue Orientale.

Because the cooking is done in bouillon, this particular fondue appeals to calorie-watchers. The service is the same as for the Fondue Bourguignonne, with the sauces being served for dipping the cooked meats. You may use any of the sauces starting on page 15.

FONDUE ORIENTALE

ASSEMBLE INGREDIENTS:
- ½ pound lean beef steak (filet or sirloin is best)
- ½ pound lean pork (loin or tenderloin)
- ½ pound veal (preferably from leg of veal and pounded thin)
- 6 veal kidneys (or lamb kidneys)
- 6 chicken livers
- 6 cups boiling beef bouillon

IN ADVANCE:

Trim meats of all fat, including the kidney. Slice into very thin bite-size pieces. If the meat is partially frozen it it easier to slice thinly. But thoroughly defrost before cooking. Prepare sauces.

AT SERVING TIME:

Provide diners with six pieces of each meat. Place the boiling chicken stock or bouillon in the fondue pot over high heat. Each diner spears a piece of meat on the fork, holds it in the boiling liquid until cooked sufficiently, switches to a cool fork and dips in one of the sauces. Keep pot boiling.

Makes 4 servings.

TIPS: You may use chicken stock or chicken bouillon (either in cans or cubes) if you prefer over beef bouillon. After the cooking is done there is a bonus. The bouillon in which the meats have been cooked is delicious and may be served to the diners in cups or refrigerated for use the following day either as is or as the basis for soup. Soy sauce, hot mustard, and sweet and sour duck sauce are especially suitable for this fondue as sauces. Make sure the chicken livers are firmly speared with the fork.

Fondue Orientale Menu

With Fondue Orientale, serve rice, a large bowl of finger relishes, mandarin oranges topped with orange sherbet, and fortune cookies.

CHINESE "HOT POT"

ASSEMBLE INGREDIENTS:

Meats:
Thinly sliced round steak
Thinly sliced boneless lamb
Boned, skinned chicken breast, thinly sliced
Shelled and deveined shrimp, split lengthwise
Scallops, cut in half
Fresh or canned oysters, drained

Vegetables:
Soybean curd, cut in ½-inch cubes (this is obtainable at Chinese stores)
Chinese or regular cabbage, shredded
Fresh spinach torn into bite-size pieces
Sliced fresh mushrooms or canned sliced mushrooms, drained
Fresh asparagus cut in 1-inch pieces
Thinly sliced fresh turnips
Cauliflower cut in bite-size pieces
Broccoli cut in bite-size pieces

Condiments:
Teriyaki sauce
Chinese oyster sauce
Soy sauce
Sharp mustard
Chutney
Barbecue sauce

1 quart hot chicken broth or beef bouillon
Cooked rice or thin noodles

IN ADVANCE:

For 4 servings, select from the above list 4 meats and/or shellfish and 3 vegetables. Select 3 or 4 condiments. Get ½ pound each of the meats selected and sufficient vegetables for four servings. If Fondue Bourguignonne plates are available, use them. Otherwise, arrange the various foods artistically on plates, one for each guest. Have condiments available so that each person may be served conveniently.

AT SERVING TIME:

In the fondue pot, over high heat, heat the broth or bouillon to boiling. The guests spear the meat and vegetables with the fondue forks, hold them in the boiling broth until they are cooked to taste, and then transfer them to another fork and eat with the desired condiment. When meat or vegetables are eaten, add the cooked rice or noodles to the broth and ladle into individual bowls.

TIPS: This is another communal meal that is fun to make and serve. With it, after the soup course, serve a fairly hearty dessert (despite the fact that this is against Chinese tradition): pecan pie and hot tea.

ANCHOVY CREAM CHEESE FONDUE

ASSEMBLE INGREDIENTS:

¼ cup capers
1 can (2 ounces) anchovy fillets
2 packages (8 ounces each) cream cheese
1¾ cups milk
2 teaspoons dry mustard
2 loaves crusty Italian or French bread cut in cubes, crust on each cube

IN ADVANCE:

Drain capers and put in a decorative small bowl. Drain anchovy fillets well, chop, and arrange in bowl with capers. Cube cream cheese.

AT SERVING TIME:

Combine cream cheese and milk in fondue pot. Place over medium heat and cook and stir until cheese is melted and blended with milk. Add mustard, capers and anchovies and continue cooking 5 minutes. To eat, spear bread with a fondue fork and dip in fondue.

Makes 6 servings.

TIPS: With Anchovy Cream Cheese Fondue serve a large bowl of finger relishes, and rum-apple pudding and coffee for dessert.

SWISS CHEESE FONDUE (made with milk)

ASSEMBLE INGREDIENTS:

3 tablespoons butter
3 tablespoons flour
1 teaspoon salt
¼ teaspoon freshly ground pepper
¼ teaspoon garlic salt
Dash of nutmeg
3 cups milk
2 packages (8 ounces each) processed Swiss cheese
2 teaspoons Worcestershire sauce
2 loaves crusty French or Italian bread cut in cubes
   with a piece of crust on each cube

AT SERVING TIME:

In a fondue pot, over medium heat, melt butter. Stir in flour, salt, pepper, garlic salt and nutmeg. Add milk gradually and cook until sauce is smooth and thickened. Lower heat and add cheese by handfuls, stirring until cheese is melted after each addition. Stir in Worcestershire sauce. To eat, spear bread with a long-handled fork and dunk in fondue. Keep hot over flame during serving.

Makes 4 servings.

TIPS: With Swiss Cheese Fondue made with milk, serve a lettuce and tomato wedge salad, dill pickles, peach pie and coffee.

LOBSTER FONDUE

ASSEMBLE INGREDIENTS:

2 cans (10 ounces) frozen condensed cream-of-shrimp soup, thawed
1 soup can milk
1 cup shredded sharp cheese (Cheddar)
1 cup cooked or canned lobster, cut up
Dash paprika
Dash cayenne
2 tablespoons sherry (optional)
1 loaf French or Italian bread cut in cubes with a piece of crust on each cube

AT SERVING TIME:

In a fondue pot, combine soup with milk and heat over low heat until mixture steams. Add cheese, lobster, paprika and cayenne. Heat, stirring often, until cheese melts and the mixture is hot and bubbly. Stir in sherry. Spear bread and dip into fondue. When the cheese has been finished the pieces of lobster may be speared and eaten.

Makes 4 servings.

SEAFOOD FONDUE

ASSEMBLE INGREDIENTS:
    1 can (13 ounces) lobster, crab or shrimp bisque
    2 tablespoons butter
    1 tablespoon chopped fresh dill (or ½ teaspoon dill
        seed)
    ½ pound natural Swiss cheese, shredded
    ⅛ teaspoon dry mustard
    Salt and freshly ground pepper to taste
    2 eggs, slightly beaten
    1 loaf French or Italian bread cut in cubes with a piece
        of crust on each cube
    32 medium-size cooked, cleaned shrimp
    Milk or cream

AT SERVING TIME:
    Heat bisque with butter and dill in fondue pot over medium heat. When thoroughly heated, but not boiling, stir in cheese a handful at a time, stirring after each addition until cheese is melted. Stir in mustard and season to taste with salt and pepper. Remove from heat and stir in eggs. Return to low heat. To eat, dunk cubes of bread and shrimp in hot sauce. If mixture thickens during serving, stir in a little milk or cream.

Makes 4 servings.

TIPS: With Seafood Fondue, serve new potatoes, romaine and green-bean salad. For dessert, meringue shells with fresh raspberries.

THE FONDUE POT
FOR ORIENTAL SOUPS

Oriental soups, like many Oriental dishes, are prepared quickly. Thus your fondue pot provides you with another way of preparing a warming dish as you chat with your guests in the living room. These delicious soups of Eastern origin can be a quickly prepared unusual prelude to a repast of roast beef, ham and chicken sandwiches following some sports occasion.

LETTUCE SOUP

ASSEMBLE INGREDIENTS:
>   4 ounces (about 1 cup) finely minced raw beef
>   1 teaspoon soy sauce
>   1 teaspoon cornstarch
>   1 teaspoon sugar
>   6 cups water
>   1 teaspoon salt
>   1 teaspoon oil
>   ½ head shredded lettuce or Chinese cabbage
>   1 cup cooked rice

IN ADVANCE:
    Soak beef in soy sauce, cornstarch and sugar.

AT SERVING TIME:

Put boiling water into a large fondue pot over high heat. Add salt, oil and beef mixture. Cook 1 minute. Add lettuce or Chinese cabbage and boil 2 minutes longer. Put a spoonful of rice in the serving cups and add the hot soup.

Makes 6 servings.

TIPS: Have all the ingredients ready on a tray and cook the soup before your guests. No one will mind if you hurry the process by starting with boiling water. The Chinese would serve only crisp fried noodles with the soup. So try this—pass a bowlful. The noodles are sprinkled on the soup. The soup course could be followed by sandwiches and potato salad. For dessert, a mixed fresh-fruit cup and cookies with coffee or hot chocolate.

CUCUMBER SOUP

ASSEMBLE INGREDIENTS:

3 cups well-seasoned chicken broth
¼ pound lean raw pork
1 large unpeeled cucumber
1 egg, slightly beaten

IN ADVANCE:

Cook chicken broth and pork for 15 minutes, covered. Remove pork from broth and cut into fine dice. Return to chicken broth. Finely dice the cucumber.

AT SERVING TIME:

Put hot chicken broth with pork in fondue pot over high heat. When boiling add cucumber and cook 3 minutes. Stir in beaten egg. Serve at once.

Makes 4 servings.

TIPS: This is easy to make, since most of the work is done in advance. Have broth in fondue pot and cucumber and egg in suitable containers on tray, along with soup bowls. Cucumber Soup might also be a good first course before barbecued chicken, vegetable casserole and a fruit-salad dessert.

CHICKEN AND MUSHROOM SOUP, JAPANESE STYLE

ASSEMBLE INGREDIENTS:
   ½ raw chicken breast, boned
   9 medium mushrooms
   5 cups well-seasoned hot chicken broth
   1 cup cooked rice
   6 strips lemon peel

IN ADVANCE:
   Cut chicken breast in thin slices. Wash mushrooms and cut in thin slices.

AT SERVING TIME:
   Put hot chicken broth in fondue pot over high heat. When boiling add chicken and mushrooms and cook for 3 minutes. To serve, put some rice and a piece of lemon peel in each bowl, add chicken and mushrooms and fill bowls with broth.

   Makes 6 servings.

TIPS: To make this soup when guests are present, put the hot broth in the fondue pot. Have chicken, mushrooms, rice and lemon in suitable containers on a tray. If you've mastered the art of chopsticks, use them to add the ingredients to the broth when it is boiling. For serving, have bowls ready. Use a slotted spoon to serve the chicken and mushrooms into the bowls and a ladle for the broth. Serve an assortment of crackers with the soup.

THE FONDUE
POT AS PUNCH BOWL

The fondue pot can be an admirable container for serving hot punch, either nonalcoholic or otherwise. Use it for small groups or be prepared to replenish the punch from the kitchen as needed, since most fondue pots are not large. The beverage recipes are planned for a 1½-quart fondue pot. For serving the hot beverages, put the fondue pot in the center of a tray large enough to also hold mugs or cups. Serve beverage with a ladle.

HOT MULLED CLARET

ASSEMBLE INGREDIENTS:
>   5 teaspoons sugar
>   ⅓ cup lemon juice
>   1 teaspoon bitters
>   1 teaspoon cinnamon
>   1 teaspoon nutmeg
>   ½ cup hot water
>   1 quart claret wine

AT SERVING TIME:
>   Mix sugar, lemon juice, bitters, spices and water and

stir to dissolve sugar. Put into fondue pot with claret and heat over medium heat until steaming but not boiling. Serve hot in mugs or cups.

Makes 8 5-ounce servings.

TIP: With Hot Mulled Claret, have a large wedge of sharp Cheddar and assorted crackers so guests can help themselves.

HOT BUTTERED RUM

ASSEMBLE INGREDIENTS:
    2 tablespoons sugar
    2 cups boiling water
    1½ cups light rum
    6 pats butter
    Nutmeg

AT SERVING TIME:
    Combine sugar and boiling water in fondue pot over high heat. Add rum and heat until steaming but not boiling. Reduce heat. Serve hot in mugs with a pat of butter and a grating of nutmeg in each serving.

Makes 6 5-ounce servings.

TIPS: Guacamole and corn chips, and miniature sliced chicken sandwiches are good with Hot Buttered Rum.

HOT TODDY

ASSEMBLE INGREDIENTS:
   2 tablespoons sugar
   2 cups boiling water
   1½ cups brandy, bourbon or rum
   4 or 5 thin lemon slices
   4 or 5 whole cloves

AT SERVING TIME:
   Combine sugar and boiling water in fondue pot over high heat. Add liquor, lemon and cloves and heat until steaming but not boiling. Reduce heat. Serve hot in mugs.

   Makes 6 5-ounce servings.

TIP: Big, fat sugar cookies and Hot Toddy seem to go together.

HOT MULLED APPLE JUICE

ASSEMBLE INGREDIENTS:
   1 quart apple juice
   ⅓ cup brown sugar
   Dash salt
   3 whole cloves
   3 whole allspice
   2 cinnamon sticks
   2 or 3 thin slices lemon

IN ADVANCE:

Simmer apple juice with brown sugar, salt and spices for about 5 minutes. Strain into fondue pot.

AT SERVING TIME:

Keep apple-juice mixture hot over low heat. Float lemon slices on top. Serve hot in mugs or cups.

Makes 6 5-ounce servings.

TIP: Doughnuts with Hot Mulled Apple Juice. What else?

HOT SPICED CRANBERRY JUICE

ASSEMBLE INGREDIENTS:
1 quart cranberry juice
1 teaspoon whole allspice
1 cinnamon stick
3 tablespoons lemon juice
3 tablespoons sugar

IN ADVANCE:

Combine all ingredients in saucepan and heat to boiling. Strain into fondue pot.

AT SERVING TIME:

Keep cranberry juice mixture hot over low heat. Serve hot in mugs or cups.

Makes 6 5-ounce servings.

TIP: Hot Spiced Cranberry Juice and miniature grilled cheese sandwiches and lots of black olives can be served together.

HOT GRAPE JUICE

ASSEMBLE INGREDIENTS:
    ½ cup sugar
    3 cups water
    6 whole cloves
    ⅓ cup lemon juice
    1 can (6 ounces) frozen grape-juice concentrate
    2 or 3 thin slices lemon

IN ADVANCE:
    Combine sugar, water and cloves in saucepan and boil
    5 minutes. Add lemon juice and grape-juice concentrate
    and reheat. Strain into fondue pot.

AT SERVING TIME:
    Keep grape-juice mixture hot over low heat. Float lemon
    slices on top. Serve hot in mugs or cups.

    Makes 6 5-ounce servings.

TIP: Serve assorted cookies with Hot Grape Juice.

HOT MULLED FRUIT PUNCH

ASSEMBLE INGREDIENTS:
    2½ cups unsweetened grapefruit juice
    2½ cups pineapple juice
    ¼ cup sugar
    2 cinnamon sticks
    1 teaspoon whole cloves

IN ADVANCE:

> Combine all ingredients in saucepan and heat to boiling. Strain into fondue pot.

AT SERVING TIME:

> Keep fruit punch hot over low heat. Serve hot in mugs or cups.

> *Makes 8 5-ounce servings.*

TIP: Serve small ham sandwiches and fresh radishes with Hot Mulled Fruit Punch.

DESSERT FONDUES

Chocolate Fondue

The Swiss are very inventive and somewhere along the way decided that since chocolate was so good with fruit and the Swiss made such good chocolate . . . why not a Chocolate Fondue? Very attractive, small fondue pots with candle warmers are primarily designed for Chocolate Fondue. Of course, you can use your regular fondue pot for this dessert and the other dessert recipes.

CHOCOLATE FONDUE

ASSEMBLE INGREDIENTS:
    6 tablespoons cream*
    3 4-ounce bars sweet cooking-chocolate
    ⅛ teaspoon cinnamon
    2 tablespoons brandy

AT SERVING TIME:
    Heat cream over low heat in a 1½-cup fondue pot.
    Break chocolate into pieces and add to cream, stirring

---

* This amount of cream makes a thick, dark chocolate sauce. Add more cream for a lighter, thinner sauce.

to make a smooth sauce as chocolate melts. Stir in cinnamon and brandy. Serve fresh fruit, such as pieces of apple, pineapple, pears and orange sections to dip in the chocolate sauce.

Makes enough for 4 servings.

TIPS: This rich chocolate sauce is kept warm in the small fondue pot. Serve a simple cookie along with the fruit. The fondue pot with the chocolate sauce should be set in the center of a suitably sized decorative tray and the fruit arranged around it, or each person may be given a small plate on which the fruit is arranged. One dips from that dish into the chocolate mixture.

FRUIT-SAUCE DIP

ASSEMBLE INGREDIENTS:

2 tablespoons cornstarch
3 tablespoons sugar
Dash salt
¾ cup cold water
3 tablespoons lemon juice
¼ cup orange juice
½ cup currant jelly
¼ cup sherry

IN ADVANCE:

Combine cornstarch, sugar, salt and water. Stir to dissolve cornstarch, then bring to a boil and cook and stir until mixture is thickened and clear. Stir in remaining ingredients.

AT SERVING TIME:

Pour into fondue pot and keep warm over low heat. Use as a dip for pieces of fresh and dried fruits.

Makes 2 cups.

TIP: Arrange fondue pot in center of tray and have dishes of pear wedges, dates, apple slices, figs, pineapple cubes and banana chunks around edge of tray to dip into the fruit sauce.

BANANA DESSERT FONDUE

ASSEMBLE INGREDIENTS:

1 cup dry white wine
½ pound natural Swiss cheese, shredded
2 tablespoons flour
Salt to taste
⅛ teaspoon freshly ground pepper
¼ teaspoon nutmeg
Bananas
Cornflake crumbs

AT SERVING TIME:

Heat wine in fondue pot over moderate heat until hot but not boiling. Dredge cheese with flour and add by handfuls to wine, stirring constantly with a wooden spoon or fork. Keep stirring until cheese is melted. Add seasonings. Cut bananas into chunks and have cornflakes in several shallow bowls. Spear banana chunks with fondue fork, dip in hot cheese mixture and then in cornflakes.

Makes 4 servings.

TIP: When you've had enough of fondue as a main course, try Banana Fondue for dessert. It is a delightful way to prolong the dinner hour when served with coffee and conversation.

Just For Fun . . .

Pretzel Surprise

For an after-dinner whimsey, melt sweet chocolate in a fondue pot over low heat and serve it with a big bowl of pretzels. It's more fun to have a variety of shapes of pretzels. Show the guests how to twirl the pretzels in the melted chocolate and then eat. It's a marvelous combination and is guaranteed to intrigue the most jaded appetite for at least a few pretzels.

THE FONDUE POT
FOR HORS D'OEUVRES

Use of a fondue pot is an excellent way of preparing and serving certain types of hot hors d'oeuvres when entertaining. While it was certainly not designed for this purpose, rather than let it sit on the shelf, press it into service.

CHILI CON QUESO DIP

ASSEMBLE INGREDIENTS:
   ¼ cup finely chopped onion
   2 tablespoons butter
   1 cup (8-ounce can) tomato sauce
   ¼ cup finely chopped green chili peppers
   ¼ pound pasteurized-process cheese spread
   Corn chips

AT SERVING TIME:
   In the fondue pot, over medium heat, cook the onion in the butter until tender. Add the tomato sauce and the chili peppers and simmer 10 minutes. Cube cheese spread and add to tomato sauce. Heat until cheese is melted. Serve hot with corn chips (or crisp tortillas).

Makes about 1½ cups.

TIPS: To serve Chili Con Queso Dip, set the fondue pot in the center of a pretty tray, large enough to hold the pot and trivet, and surround the base with corn chips or crisp tortillas. Pile a stack of small napkins near it.

PERROS CALIENTES

ASSEMBLE INGREDIENTS:
>   2 cups barbecue sauce
>   1 pound frankfurters cut in 1-inch pieces

AT SERVING TIME:
>   Heat barbecue sauce with frankfurter pieces. Spoon sauce and frankfurters into fondue pot and keep hot over low heat. Serve with picks.

Makes about 45 pieces.

TIPS: Use your own barbecue-sauce recipe or the one on page 19 (Western Sauce). If in a hurry, there are prepared sauces on the market that can be used as is or spiced with a touch of Tabasco or Worcestershire sauce to give you almost instant hors d'oeuvres.

HOT CHILI CHEESE DIP

ASSEMBLE INGREDIENTS:
>   1 package (8 ounces) cream cheese
>   1 can (10¾ ounces) condensed tomato soup
>   1 tablespoon instant minced onion
>   1½ teaspoons chili powder
>   ½ teaspoon Tabasco
>   1 package (2 pounds) frozen French-fried potatoes, prepared as directed

AT SERVING TIME:

Cut the cream cheese into 8 cubes. Combine with tomato soup and instant minced onion in the fondue pot and stir over medium heat until the cheese melts and is blended with the soup. Add seasonings. Serve hot with crisp French-fried potatoes.

Makes 2 cups.

TIP: To serve this Hot Chili Cheese Dip, put the hot French-fries in a napkin-lined basket or in an electric bun warmer and place them near the fondue pot.

HOT MARINATED ARTICHOKE HEARTS

ASSEMBLE INGREDIENTS:

2 packages (9 ounces each) frozen deluxe artichoke hearts
1 cup peanut oil
⅓ cup tarragon vinegar
½ teaspoon salt
¼ teaspoon freshly ground pepper
1 teaspoon prepared strong mustard
2 teaspoons minced green onion
2 tablespoons minced parsley
1 clove garlic, quartered

IN ADVANCE:

Cook artichokes as directed on package. Do not over-cook. Drain.

AT SERVING TIME:

Combine artichokes with oil, vinegar, and seasonings in

fondue pot and heat until steaming. Hold over low heat during serving. Serve with picks.

Makes about 2½ cups.

TIP: If there are any artichokes left over, don't throw them out. They are wonderful chilled, too.

FRESH VEGETABLE RELISHES WITH SWISS CHEESE FONDUE

ASSEMBLE INGREDIENTS:
> 1 pound natural Swiss cheese
> 1 tablespoon flour
> 1 clove garlic, cut in half
> ¾ cup dry white wine
> ½ teaspoon salt
> Mace and freshly ground pepper to taste
> Flowerets of cauliflower, broccoli, celery and carrot sticks, and radishes

IN ADVANCE:
> Shred cheese and toss with flour.

AT SERVING TIME:
> Rub inside of fondue pot with cut clove of garlic. Pour in wine and heat until air bubbles rise to the surface but do not boil. Gradually add cheese-flour mixture, stirring until cheese is completely melted. Season with salt, pepper and mace as desired. Keep hot over low heat. Mixture is somewhat thick and stringy. If during serving it becomes too thick, thin with a little additional dry white wine.

Makes 2 cups sauce.

TIP: Center fondue pot and trivet on large tray and surround with an artistic arrangement of the raw vegetable relishes.

QUICK FONDUE DIP

ASSEMBLE INGREDIENTS:

    1 can (10¾ ounces) condensed Cheddar-cheese soup
    2 slices (2 ounces) natural Swiss cheese, cut up
    1 medium clove garlic, minced
    2 tablespoons Chablis or other dry white wine
    1 loaf French or Italian bread cut in cubes with a piece of crust on each cube

AT SERVING TIME:

In a fondue pot over medium heat combine all ingredients except bread. Heat and stir occasionally until cheese melts and mixture is thoroughly heated. Spear bread with a toothpick or a fork and dip into fondue.

Makes 1½ cups.

TIPS: When you're in a hurry and want to have a tasty hot dip, this is the perfect answer. It might even be worth your while to keep these ingredients on hand as part of the emergency shelf. French bread freezes well and defrosts quickly.

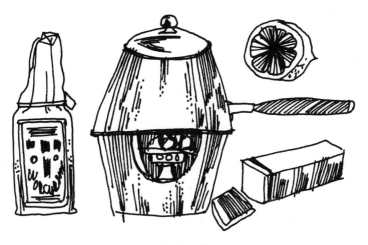

QUICK CHEDDAR DIP

ASSEMBLE INGREDIENTS:
> 2 cans (10¾ ounces each) condensed Cheddar-cheese
>   soup
> 1 tablespoon Worcestershire sauce
> 3 teaspoons lemon juice
> 2 tablespoons frozen chopped chives
> ½ loaf French or Italian bread cut in cubes with a piece
>   of crust on each cube

AT SERVING TIME:
> Combine soup with Worcestershire sauce and lemon
> juice in fondue pot over medium heat. Stir occasionally
> until mixture is hot. Mix in chives. To eat, dunk pieces
> of bread in cheese mixture.
>
> *Makes about 2½ cups.*

TIPS: This tasty quickie is worth keeping on a pantry shelf at
the ready. If French bread is not on hand, use corn chips or
potato-chip crackers for dipping.

2.
THE
CHAFING DISH

———————————

The chafing dish is the showpiece of the world of pots and pans. Elegantly graceful in design, this is one kind of cookware that does not hide in the kitchen but presides graciously at table or buffet, even when not in use. In the Victorian era the use of the chafing dish became almost a cult and elaborate accessories were part of the vogue. Small cabinets were designed to hold spices, other groceries, liquors and cooking implements, as well as fuel for the heating lamp. The expert in the use of the chafing dish was as proud of his skill as our barbecue chefs are today. Well-bred young ladies of that time learned to cook at least one chafing-dish specialty for their beaux, even if they knew nothing else of the culinary arts.

Once again the chafing dish has become popular. And a most gratifying situation it is, for this versatile piece of equipment has many uses. Chief among them is its ability to add a warm, convivial atmosphere to a party. Conceivably, the skilled performer at the chafing dish could begin the dinner with Hot Clams, continue with Salmis of Duck, carry on with Cherries Jubilee and end with Café Brûlot. With a little blazer pan washing and refueling along the way, the diners would be well fed even if they might have to wait for the chef.

The word "chafing" derives from the French *chauffer*—"to make warm." Many purists of chafing-dish cookery might quibble with the use of a chafing dish just for keeping foods warm that have not been cooked in it. But very often at large parties it is not practical to cook in the dining or living room, although most convenient to have hot hors d'oeuvres available in the warming chafing dish.

A chafing dish, as contrasted with other tabletop cookware, always has two pans: one, to hold water, is placed directly over the heat source; the other, set over the water pan, is called the blazer. The blazer pan has a lid. Both pans fit into a trivet, which holds the heat source. This heat source may be an alcohol burner, Sterno, a butane-gas burner or electricity. In chafing-dish cookery, foods may be sautéed in the blazer pan over direct heat. The heat source also keeps the water in the water pan hot or boiling.

Heat adjustments for the chafing dish depend on the type of heat. Butane gas is regulated by a dial or lever. Denatured-alcohol burners are adjusted by air holes in the lid while a canned-fuel container has a lid that swings open or shut to adjust the amount of heat released. An electrically heated chafing dish may or may not have a temperature control. Heat adjustment is important when cooking over direct heat in the blazer pan and to control the temperature of the water in the water pan.

The majority of chafing dishes are made of metal. Copper is the most popular. They come in sizes ranging from 2 pints to several quarts, which indicate the liquid measure of the blazer pan. If one wants to do a great deal of chafing-dish cooking, more than one chafing dish is usually required. A very rich dessert sauce would be made in much smaller quantities, for example, than a main course.

The blazer pan is also made in different shapes for various uses. A flat pan is more efficient for cooking Crêpes Suzette and omelets, while a pan with greater depth is used for other types of food. However, don't let the lack of a flat pan keep you from making Crêpes Suzette. They can be prepared in advance and heated with the sauce and glazed in the regular chafing-dish blazer.

If you are selecting your own chafing dish, think of the kinds of food to be cooked in it and then buy accordingly. If it is to be used mainly for main-dish entertaining, get one large enough to accommodate your favorite recipes. If your forte is to be dessert sauces, perhaps a smaller dish will do.

Some chafing dishes are made so that the water pan cannot be removed from the trivet. If yours is of this kind, a small amount of sautéing over direct heat can be done at the kitchen range and the recipe finished at the chafing dish. If one has a butane burner with its own trivet, this can be used as an adjunct to the chafing dish for cooking in the blazer pan over direct heat. If you own this type of chafing dish, experiment and find the recipes that suit it best.

SOME GENERAL HINTS
WHEN COOKING
BEFORE GUESTS

Always practice a recipe in private or for your family at least once before the public performance.

When readying things for the performance, be sure that the conditions of the practice session (if successful) are duplicated as nearly as possible; *i.e.,* if all ingredients came directly from the refrigerator or if they were at room temperature, duplicate for the final.

Check the heat source for sufficient fuel to carry through the cooking and serving. Have extra fuel ready.

Have all the ingredients ready on a tray in the order in which they are added to the blazer pan.

Do absolutely everything necessary to make your performance look extremely skillful.

Keep the chafing dish out of a direct draft or breeze.

If you intend to do a great deal of cooking in front of guests, invest in some interesting accessories. A handsome pepper mill; colorful bowls to hold ingredients such as chopped onions or seasonings such as chili sauce; and small pitchers for liquids will add to the total picture and make it much more attractive.

58

HORS D'OEUVRES

You can set a dramatic scene for the service of hors d'oeuvres by using the chafing dish. For intimate gatherings, it is fun to actually prepare the food before the guests. For larger parties, the chafing dish serves the logical purpose of keeping hot hors d'oeuvres hot. It may be preferable to prepare hot hors d'oeuvres in advance in the kitchen and use the chafing dish just as a serving convenience. Don't apologize for this. No cooking utensil should be the master of its owner, so use the chafing dish as it suits you. In any event, it will add grace to the party. Chafing-dish appetizers are often less work than the cold offerings someone slaved over for hours and are more highly esteemed by guests.

When hot appetizers are being served from the chafing dish, put a pile of small plates near it. This makes it easier for a guest to serve himself and cuts down on the possibility of misfortune to the rugs. Today there are many handsome patterns of plastic-coated paper plates, which add to the color of the party and are quite proper. Also include a stack of small napkins for the person who doesn't want a plate but should have a little protection!

OYSTER FRY

ASSEMBLE INGREDIENTS:
   2 dozen small oysters
   ¼ teaspoon salt
   ⅛ teaspoon freshly ground pepper
   3 tablespoons flour
   3 to 4 tablespoons butter
   1 teaspoon Worcestershire sauce
   1 teaspoon lemon juice
   2 tablespoons chopped parsley
   2 dozen toast rounds

IN ADVANCE:
   Drain oysters and pat dry on paper towels.

AT SERVING TIME:
   Season with salt and pepper and dip in flour. Melt butter in blazer pan over moderate heat, using just enough to cover bottom of pan. Add oysters and brown on both sides. Stir in Worcestershire sauce and lemon juice and heat thoroughly. Sprinkle with chopped parsley. Serve hot oysters on toast rounds at once.

   Makes 2 dozen.

TIPS: To prepare this dish before guests, have drained and dried oysters on linen napkin on plate. Salt, pepper and flour should be on a small plate. Use tongs or long-handled fork for handling the oysters during the flouring and frying. Flour the oysters while the butter is heating in the blazer. Have the toast rounds ready in a napkin-lined basket.

SAUTÉED MUSHROOMS

ASSEMBLE INGREDIENTS:

    1 dozen medium-sized whole fresh mushrooms
    ½ teaspoon salt
    Dash freshly ground pepper
    ¼ teaspoon paprika
    2 to 3 tablespoons butter
    1 tablespoon chopped chives

IN ADVANCE:

Wash, dry and remove stems from mushrooms. Season with salt, pepper and paprika and put into a decorative bowl.

AT SERVING TIME:

Heat butter in blazer pan over moderate heat. Add seasoned mushrooms and sauté until lightly browned. Sprinkle with chives. Serve at once or keep hot over hot water in water pan.

Makes 1 dozen.

TIP: Don't prepare the mushrooms more than an hour or two in advance. The mushrooms only take about 3 minutes to cook, so this can wait until the last minute to prepare.

EGGS SMOLAND

ASSEMBLE INGREDIENTS:

    6 hard cooked eggs
    6 anchovy fillets
    1½ tablespoons butter
    ½ cup finely chopped onion
    1 tablespoon finely chopped parsley
    1½ dozen toast rounds

IN ADVANCE:
Finely chop eggs and anchovy fillets.

AT SERVING TIME:
Heat butter in blazer pan over moderate heat. Add onions and cook and stir until onions are tender but not browned. Stir in eggs, anchovies and parsley. Put over hot water in pan to heat and keep hot. Serve heaped on toast rounds.

Makes 1½ dozen.

TIPS: On tray, have one bowl with chopped eggs, smaller bowls with chopped anchovy, parsley and onions. Stir mixture with a wooden spoon while cooking. Use a stainless-steel spoon for serving. Have toast rounds in a napkin-lined basket.

HOT CRAB CANAPÉS

ASSEMBLE INGREDIENTS:
    ½ pound crab meat
    3 tablespoons butter
    2 tablespoons flour
    ½ teaspoon salt
    Dash freshly ground pepper
    1½ cups half milk, half cream
    ½ teaspoon paprika
    ¼ cup dry sherry
    2 tablespoons butter
    3½ dozen toast rounds

IN ADVANCE:
Flake crab meat and remove any cartilage and shell.

AT SERVING TIME:

Heat 3 tablespoons butter in blazer pan over moderate heat. Stir in flour, salt, and pepper and let bubble. Stir in half-and-half and cook and stir until mixture boils and is thickened. Place over hot water in water pan and stir in crab meat, paprika, sherry, remaining butter. Cook until mixture is thoroughly heated. Serve on toast rounds.

Makes 3½ dozen.

TIP: To make canapés that have a cream-sauce base, use a pitcher, about 2- to 3-cup size, that pours without spilling for adding the liquid to the flour-butter mixture.

DEVILED CHICKEN

ASSEMBLE INGREDIENTS:

2 tablespoons butter
2 tablespoons flour
½ cup chicken stock
½ cup cream or undiluted evaporated milk
1 teaspoon Worcestershire sauce
½ clove garlic, crushed
½ teaspoon prepared mustard
Salt and freshly ground pepper to taste
¼ cup dry sherry
2 cups finely minced cooked chicken
Assorted fresh-vegetable relishes or crisp crackers

AT SERVING TIME:

Heat butter in blazer pan over moderate heat. Stir in flour, chicken stock, cream and seasonings. Cook and stir until mixture is thickened and smooth. Stir in sherry and chicken. Place over boiling water in water pan and heat, stirring occasionally. Serve as a dip for assorted fresh relishes, such as cucumber slices, carrot curls, celery sticks, turnip slices or crisp crackers.

Makes 2½ cups.

TIPS: Deviled Chicken served with assorted fresh vegetables is an unusual but very good combination. One of the virtues of this dish, besides its good flavor, is that it is a pantry-shelf recipe, since everything that is in it can be kept ready for the unexpected.

BLAZING CHICKEN LIVERS

ASSEMBLE INGREDIENTS:
> 2 tablespoons butter
> 1 dozen chicken livers cut in bite-size pieces
> 2 tablespoons flour
> ½ teaspoon salt
> Dash of freshly ground pepper
> ¼ cup warm brandy (cognac)
> 2 dozen toast rounds

AT SERVING TIME:
> Heat butter in blazer pan over moderate heat. Sprinkle flour, salt and pepper over chicken livers and sauté quickly on all sides. Pour brandy over chicken livers and ignite. When blaze has burned out, put pan of chicken

livers over hot water in water pan to keep hot while serving. Serve on toast rounds.

Makes 2 dozen servings.

TIPS: Chicken livers are better if not overcooked, so this operation should be a fast one. If you neglect to warm the brandy, let the brandy warm with the chicken livers before igniting. Be sure to have matches on the tray with the other items. Long-handled fireplace matches are perfect for this job.

STEAK BITS

ASSEMBLE INGREDIENTS:
   2 tablespoons butter
   ½ clove garlic, crushed
   ½ pound top sirloin steak cut in thin bite-size pieces
   ½ teaspoon salt
   Dash of freshly ground pepper
   1½ dozen slices buttered party or icebox rye bread

AT SERVING TIME:
   Heat butter and garlic in blazer pan over high heat. Season steak with salt and pepper and quickly sauté pieces as needed on all sides. Serve at once on buttered rye bread.

Makes 1½ dozen servings.

TIPS: This is a very basic hors d'oeuvre that appeals to most everyone. It's better not to cook too many at once, as the butter cools off and the meat just stews in its own juice. This recipe can be "gussied up" with 1 teaspoon of brown steak sauce and ½ teaspoon prepared mustard to make miniature Steak Diables if one wishes.

LOBSTER MADRID

ASSEMBLE INGREDIENTS:
  1 can (5 ounces) lobster meat or ⅔ cup fresh lobster
     meat
  3 tablespoons sweet sherry
  2 tablespoons butter
  ½ cup chili sauce
  ½ teaspoon salt
  Dash cayenne
  1 tablespoon Worcestershire sauce
  1½ dozen toast rounds or crackers

IN ADVANCE:
  Drain and flake lobster. Combine with sherry and let
  stand for 30 minutes or longer.

AT SERVING TIME:
  Heat butter in blazer pan over boiling water. Add chili
  sauce, salt, cayenne and Worcestershire sauce. Cook,
  stirring occasionally, until mixture is hot and flavors are
  blended. Add marinated lobster meat. When heated
  through, serve on toast rounds.

  Makes 1½ dozen servings.

TIPS: Lobster Madrid is a favorite, so make plenty. If cayenne pepper is not one of your favorite spices, use a little Tabasco instead or omit altogether and use freshly ground pepper. There is nothing complicated about making this dish before guests. Just be sure it is piping hot before serving.

PEPPER EGGS

ASSEMBLE INGREDIENTS:
    3 green peppers
    6 eggs
    6 tablespoons water
    ½ teaspoon salt
    ½ teaspoon chili powder
    Dash cumin
    ½ cup shredded sharp Cheddar cheese
    2 tablespoons butter

IN ADVANCE:
    Wash and remove seeds from pepper. Cut into 1½-inch squares. Lightly beat eggs with water and seasonings. Fold in cheese.

AT SERVING TIME:
    Heat butter in blazer pan over moderate heat. Add egg mixture to melted butter and cook and stir until eggs are just set. Put over hot water in water pan. Surround eggs with squares of green pepper. Guests serve themselves by dishing up some egg mixture on green-pepper squares.

    Makes about 1½ dozen servings.

TIPS: Stir eggs with a wooden spoon during cooking. Serve with a stainless-steel spoon. Undercook the eggs if they will be over hot water for any length of time. This is a simple but marvelous flavor, color and texture combination. Everyone will think you're terribly clever to make something so tasty from everyday foods.

HOT CLAMS

ASSEMBLE INGREDIENTS:
    3 dozen large clams in the shell
    Bottled clam juice
    2 tablespoons butter
    ¼ cup finely chopped onion
    ¼ cup finely chopped pimiento
    1 clove garlic, mashed
    ½ teaspoon salt
    Dash of freshly ground pepper
    Toast squares

IN ADVANCE:
    Scrub clam shells well. Open clams and remove. Save
    and measure clam liquor. Add enough additional clam
    juice to make 1¼ cups if necessary.

AT SERVING TIME:
    Heat butter in blazer pan over medium heat. Add onion
    and sauté until tender. Add pimiento, garlic, clams,
    clam juice and salt and pepper. Bring to a boil and place
    over hot water in pan and cook for 5 minutes. Serve
    clams on toast squares.

    Makes 36 servings.

TIPS: Have the toast squares in a napkin-lined basket and a
plate of lemon wedges nearby. Some people like to squeeze
a little lemon on the clams. This is a particularly good appe-
tizer to serve for a brunch party. There is nothing complicated
about preparing this dish before the guests, just be sure all
ingredients are conveniently arranged on the tray in containers.

HERBED SHRIMP

ASSEMBLE INGREDIENTS:
¼ cup butter
2 tablespoons chopped parsley
1 teaspoon chopped chives
1 teaspoon dried dill weed
1 pound cleaned raw shrimp
¼ teaspoon salt
Dash Tabasco
1 tablespoon sherry
1 tablespoon lemon juice

AT SERVING TIME:
Heat butter in blazer pan over moderate heat with parsley, chives and dill. Add shrimp and sprinkle with salt and Tabasco. Cook for 5 minutes, turning once. Add sherry and lemon juice. Place over hot water in pan and keep hot to serve. Serve with picks.

Makes 3 to 4 dozen medium shrimp.

TIPS: To cook this dish before guests, be sure that the raw (green) shrimp are well dried. If they have too much moisture clinging to them, they will stew in the blazer pan rather than cook neatly as they should. Have everything ready on the tray and speed ahead. It's fun to watch the shrimp turn from a rather homely gray to a pretty pink.

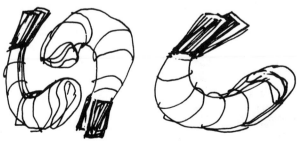

CURRIED CHEESE SHRIMP

ASSEMBLE INGREDIENTS:
>   2 packages (8 ounces each) Neufchâtel cheese
>   ¼ cup lemon juice
>   ⅔ cup milk
>   1½ teaspoons curry powder
>   ½ teaspoon salt
>   4 cups cooked, cleaned shrimp
>   Round buttery crackers

IN ADVANCE:
>   Soften cheese at room temperature.

AT SERVING TIME:
>   Blend lemon juice, milk, curry powder and salt into cheese in blazer pan. Set over hot water in pan and cook until cheese is melted and mixture blended and hot, stirring occasionally. Add shrimp. Cover and cook until shrimp is hot, stirring occasionally. Spear with picks and serve on cracker.

Makes about 3 dozen, depending on size of shrimps.

TIPS: Anyone who has stared at cold cooked shrimp with cocktail sauce at parties will enjoy Cheese Shrimp as a change. For the cold-shrimp holdouts, serve both.

COCKTAIL CURRY DIP

ASSEMBLE INGREDIENTS:
- ¼ cup butter
- 1 green onion, minced
- 2 tablespoons flour
- 3 tablespoons chopped crystallized ginger (or 1 teaspoon minced ginger root)
- ½ cup chopped peeled apple
- 1 to 2 teaspoons curry powder
- 1 teaspoon salt
- 1 teaspoon sugar
- ⅛ teaspoon ground cloves
- Dash cayenne
- 2 cups milk
- ½ cup moist shredded coconut
- ¼ cup lemon juice
- Cream
- Flowerets of cauliflower, broccoli, zucchini and celery sticks; carrot and pepper slices; and radishes and cherry tomatoes

IN ADVANCE:

Heat butter in skillet and sauté onion until tender, stirring. Blend in flour and when mixture bubbles, add ginger, apple, curry, salt, sugar, clove and cayenne. Slowly stir in milk. Cook and stir until sauce thickens. Cover and cook over low heat 30 minutes. Chill.

AT SERVING TIME:

Put chilled sauce into blazer pan and set over hot water in pan. When thoroughly hot, add coconut and lemon juice. Cream may be added if consistency is too thick. Serve with vegetables for dipping.

Makes 3 cups.

TIPS: Cocktail Curry Dip may sound rather complicated to prepare, but, besides being good, it has the virtue of any dip that can be prepared in advance. The spicy curry flavor, with the fresh crisp vegetables, is a delightful change from the usual canapes. Whenever fresh vegetables are used with a dip, arrange them with an eye to their decorative possibilities.

SAUSAGE ÉLÉGANTE

ASSEMBLE INGREDIENTS:
   1 pound link sausage
   ⅓ cup light brown sugar
   ⅓ cup soy sauce
   ½ cup warm, light rum

IN ADVANCE:
   Cut sausages into thirds or fourths. Sauté in skillet until done. Drain off fat.

AT SERVING TIME:
   Transfer cooked sausages to blazer pan. Add sugar and soy sauce. Stir and cook over hot water in water pan for about 2 minutes. Add rum and ignite. Serve hot on picks.

   Makes about 3½ dozen.

TIPS: Save the blazing until the guests arrive, but browning the sausages and decanting the fat can be more easily done in the kitchen. If you feel the need of a dip for the sausages, have a little pot of hot mustard available. Don't forget the long matches for igniting the rum.

PARTY BEEFBURGERS

ASSEMBLE INGREDIENTS:

Burgers:

1 egg, beaten

¼ cup milk

¾ cup bite-size toasted corn cereal, crushed

¾ teaspoon poultry seasoning

½ teaspoon seasoned salt

⅛ teaspoon freshly ground pepper

¼ cup chopped onion

1 pound ground beef chuck

Butter or margarine

Sauce:

1 can condensed cream-of-chicken soup

½ soup-can milk

IN ADVANCE:

Mix egg with ¼ cup milk, cereal and seasonings. Add beef and mix well. Shape into 2 dozen small hamburgers and brown in a small amount of fat in a skillet, turning to brown all sides. Pour off excess fat. Mix soup with ½ soup-can milk and pour over hamburgers. Cover and cook over low heat 30 minutes.

AT SERVING TIME:

Transfer hamburgers and sauce to blazer pan set over boiling water. Serve with picks.

Makes 2 dozen.

TIPS: Everyone likes miniature meatballs, and this is an interesting recipe and sauce. Crackers or toast rounds can also be served with the tiny burgers.

SPICY POTATO MEATBALLS

ASSEMBLE INGREDIENTS:
  1 cup mashed potatoes (may use instant type)
  1 pound ground beef chuck
  ½ pound ground fresh pork
  1 egg
  2 tablespoons minced onion
  1 teaspoon sugar
  1 teaspoon salt
  ¼ teaspoon nutmeg
  ⅛ teaspoon allspice
  ⅛ teaspoon ginger
  Butter or shortening
  Chili sauce (optional)

IN ADVANCE:

Prepare mashed potatoes. Add remaining ingredients, except butter and chili sauce, and mix thoroughly. Form into 48 small meatballs. Heat butter or shortening in skillet and brown meatballs on all sides over low heat until thoroughly cooked.

AT SERVING TIME:

Transfer meatballs to blazer pan and keep hot over water pan. Serve with picks. If desired, a dish of chili sauce may be used for a dip.

Makes 4 dozen.

TIP: Small meatballs are easier to fry if first dipped in flour.

BRANDIED BEEF D'OEUVRES

ASSEMBLE INGREDIENTS:

Meatballs:
1 pound ground beef chuck
½ cup soft breadcrumbs
1 teaspoon salt
¼ teaspoon freshly ground pepper
1 teaspoon minced onion
1 egg
Dash of paprika

IN ADVANCE:

Combine ground beef with remaining ingredients except paprika, mixing lightly. Form into 36 small meatballs. Place on greased flat baking pan. Bake in a moderate oven (400° F.) 15 minutes. Sprinkle with paprika.

ASSEMBLE INGREDIENTS:

Cherry Brandied Sauce:
¾ cup red currant jelly
2 teaspoons vinegar
¼ teaspoon Tabasco
1 tablespoon cornstarch
½ cup cherry brandy

AT SERVING TIME:

In the blazer pan, combine jelly, vinegar, Tabasco and cornstarch. Cook over low heat, stirring constantly until slightly thickened. Add the cherry brandy. Place over boiling water in water pan and add the meatballs. Heat, stirring occasionally. When hot, serve with picks.

Makes 36 meatballs.

TIP: Tuck some sprigs of crisp fresh parsley around the edge of the pan.

FLAMING WALNUT PÂTÉ BALLS

ASSEMBLE INGREDIENTS:
1 cup butter
½ teaspoon curry powder
½ cup chopped green onion
2 pounds chicken livers
Seasoned salt
1 cup chopped walnuts
2 tablespoons finely chopped parsley
⅓ cup brandy
Crackers or melba-toast rounds

IN ADVANCE:
Heat ⅓ cup butter with curry powder in skillet until bubbly. Add onion and chicken livers. Cook over low heat until chicken livers lose their pinkness and are done. Mash or sieve chicken liver mixture (or whirl smooth in blender), beating in ⅓ cup butter until smooth and well blended. Taste and add seasoned salt as desired. Refrigerate several hours or overnight. When ready to serve, shape into balls (about 36) the size of a small walnut and roll in chopped walnuts. Heat remaining ⅓ cup butter in a large skillet. Add chicken-liver balls and

cook quickly, shaking pan gently to turn and brown on all sides.

AT SERVING TIME:

Place hot Walnut Pâté Balls in blazer pan and set over water pan. Sprinkle on parsley; add brandy and warm. Flame. Serve hot with crackers or melba-toast rounds.

Makes 3 dozen.

TIP: This is a unique flavor and texture combination. The Pâté Balls can be made a day in advance if one wishes.

MAIN COURSES
IN THE CHAFING DISH

Many of the main dishes prepared or served in a chafing dish are in some kind of sauce. This often means serving over rice, toast, noodles or in patty shells. With a small party no problem arises, because the accompaniment may be brought to the table at the time of serving.

However, if you are having a buffet for a large group and the serving time may stretch over a longer period, some arrangements should be made for keeping the accompanying food hot. There are a number of electric warming trays on the market that serve this purpose. One of these might be used in conjunction with the chafing dish. A heatproof casserole filled with rice or noodles, or a platter with toast or patty shells, can be set on the warming tray. A second chafing dish might also be utilized.

At a buffet, the plates should be placed nearest the food that goes on the plate first. Keep silverware to a minimum, placing on the table only that which is absolutely necessary. Do everything possible to make service easy for the guests, such as serving prebuttered rolls and easily served salads. Individual trays are a thoughtful accessory.

Welsh Rabbit, of English origin, is to the chafing dish what the Swiss Cheese Fondue is to the fondue pot. There has always been a controversy over the name: whether it is "Rabbit" or "Rarebit." Substantial research has failed to turn up a definitive answer. An English cookery book of 1861 gives a recipe for Welsh Rarebit as simply cheese melted on pieces of toast, with no mention of today's version. The current preferred spelling is "Rabbit."

WELSH RABBIT

ASSEMBLE INGREDIENTS:

¾ pound mild or sharp Cheddar cheese, shredded
1 teaspoon dry mustard
Few grains cayenne
½ teaspoon paprika
½ teaspoon salt
½ cup beer
4 pieces toast

AT SERVING TIME:

Mix cheese with seasonings in blazer pan. Set over hot water in pan and cook, stirring until cheese begins to melt. Gradually stir in beer and continue cooking over low heat until smooth, stirring constantly. Serve hot over toast.

Makes 4 servings.

VARIATIONS:

1. *Golden Buck:* Garnish each portion of Welsh Rabbit with one poached egg.
2. *Yorkshire Buck:* Garnish each portion of Welsh Rabbit with one poached egg and slices of broiled bacon.

TIPS: Welsh Rabbit is an ideal late-supper dish. Buttered asparagus spears, thick slices of fresh tomato seasoned with fresh herbs and oil and vinegar, beer or ale, and lemon sherbet with pecan cookies for dessert could complete the menu.

SHRIMP RABBIT

ASSEMBLE INGREDIENTS:
   ¼ cup butter
   ¼ cup flour
   1¼ teaspoons salt
   2 cups milk
   1 teaspoon Worcestershire sauce
   Dash Tabasco
   2 cups shredded American cheese (½ pound)
   1½ cups cooked shrimp
   4 pieces toast

AT SERVING TIME:
   Heat butter in blazer pan over moderate heat. Add flour
   and salt and stir until bubbly. Set over hot water in pan
   and stir in milk. Cook until mixture is thickened, stirring
   occasionally. Add Worcestershire, Tabasco and cheese.
   Stir until cheese melts. Add shrimp and heat. Serve hot
   over toast.

   Makes 4 servings.

TIPS: With Shrimp Rabbit serve green beans cooked with
tiny cocktail onions, and a wedge of lettuce with Thousand
Island dressing. For dessert serve strawberries over ice cream,
and hot coffee.

TOMATO RABBIT

ASSEMBLE INGREDIENTS:
   4 tablespoons butter
   ⅓ cup chopped onion
   ⅓ cup chopped green pepper
   ⅓ cup chopped celery
   2 tablespoons flour
   1 cup milk
   2 cups shredded American or Cheddar cheese
   ½ teaspoon salt
   ½ teaspoon chili powder
   1 cup canned tomatoes
   4 English muffins, split and toasted

AT SERVING TIME:
   Heat butter in blazer pan over moderate heat. Add onion, green pepper and celery and cook and stir until tender but not browned. Stir in flour and let bubble. Place pan over hot water in water pan and slowly stir in milk. Cook until mixture is thickened, stirring occasionally. Add cheese and seasonings and stir until cheese is melted. Add tomatoes and cook and stir until heated. Serve over split and toasted English muffins.

   Makes 4 servings.

TIPS: With Tomato Rabbit serve a large bowl of fresh-vegetable relishes, more toasted English muffins, and fresh pineapple for dessert.

LOBSTER RABBIT

ASSEMBLE INGREDIENTS:

   6 2-ounce rock-lobster tails, frozen
   1¼ cups undiluted evaporated milk
   2½ tablespoons tomato paste
   ¾ pound shredded sharp natural Cheddar cheese
   ¼ teaspoon basil
   ½ teaspoon salt
   4 pieces toast

IN ADVANCE:

Drop frozen rock-lobster tails into boiling salted water to cover and cook for 2 minutes after water reboils. Drain immediately and cool under running cold water. Cut away underside membrane and remove meat in one piece. Slice tail meat into medallions crosswise.

AT SERVING TIME:

Mix evaporated milk with tomato paste in the blazer pan and place over hot water in water pan. Heat until mixture steams, stirring occasionally. Add cheese by handfuls, stirring after each addition until melted. Stir in basil, salt and lobster meat. Reheat. Serve on toast.

Makes 4 servings.

TIPS: A salad of sliced pickled beets with thinly sliced onion and crisp lettuce, hot homemade rolls, chilled dry white wine, and a bowl of fresh fruit with crisp cookies for dessert could complete the menu.

BEAN RABBIT

ASSEMBLE INGREDIENTS:

2 cups cold baked beans
¼ cup butter
½ teaspoon paprika
1 teaspoon salt
1½ cups milk
1½ cups shredded natural sharp Cheddar cheese
Toasted pilot crackers

IN ADVANCE:

In a small bowl mash beans with a fork.

AT SERVING TIME:

Heat butter in blazer pan over moderate heat. Stir in seasonings and beans. When hot, add milk and cheese and place over boiling water in pan. Cook, stirring occasionally, until cheese is melted and mixture is hot. Serve on toasted pilot crackers.

Makes 4 servings.

TIPS: Bean Rabbit, to the uninitiated, may sound like too much, but it's truly a very good combination. Plan it for a Sunday supper and serve celery slaw and baked apples for dessert with it.

ONION RABBIT

ASSEMBLE INGREDIENTS:

1 can (10¾ ounces) condensed onion soup
½ pound shredded natural Cheddar cheese
½ teaspoon dry mustard
½ cup dry red wine
2 pieces toast

AT SERVING TIME:

Heat onion soup in blazer pan over moderate heat. When steaming, place over hot water in pan. Stir in cheese, mustard and wine. Cook and stir until cheese is melted and mixture is smooth and hot. Serve over toast.

Makes 2 servings.

TIPS: This quickie is ideal for a cold winter night late supper. Serve with beer and pickles and finish with a fresh-fruit tray.

SUPPER SOUP

ASSEMBLE INGREDIENTS:

1 tablespoon butter
½ pound ground beef chuck
4 tablespoons chopped onion
1½ teaspoons chili powder
½ teaspoon salt
1 can (10¾ ounces) condensed tomato soup
1 can (10¾ ounces) condensed beef bouillon
1½ soup-cans water

AT SERVING TIME:

Heat butter in blazer pan over moderate heat and brown beef and onion, stirring. Add remaining ingredients and bring to a boil. Place over boiling water in pan. Cover and simmer for 15 or 20 minutes, stirring often.

Makes 4 servings.

TIPS: A good Sunday night light-supper dish. Serve lots of crisp crackers and a hearty dessert, such as apple dumplings, with it. Since this soup cooks for 15 to 20 minutes, one might prepare it on the range and reheat and serve in the chafing dish.

CHEESE SOUP

ASSEMBLE INGREDIENTS:
> ¼ cup butter
> 2 tablespoons minced onion
> ½ cup thinly sliced carrot
> ¾ cup finely chopped celery
> 1 cup chicken broth (or 1 cup water and 1 chicken-
>   bouillon cube)
> ¼ cup flour
> 3 cups milk
> 2 cups shredded Cheddar cheese
> Finely chopped parsley

AT SERVING TIME:
> Heat butter in blazer pan over moderate heat. Add on-
> ion, carrot and celery and cook until vegetables are
> tender, stirring often. Add broth and bring to a boil.
> Place over boiling water in pan. Mix flour with one cup
> milk to form a thin paste and stir into the vegetable-
> broth mixture. Cook until thickened. Add cheese and
> stir until melted, then gradually stir in remaining milk.
> Heat to serving temperature, stirring. Garnish each bowl
> with parsley.

Makes 4 hearty servings.

TIPS: Serve with hot, buttered crusty bread, vegetable relishes, and chilled pear halves with a touch of ginger brandy.

LOBSTER SOUP

ASSEMBLE INGREDIENTS:
> 1 can (10¾ ounces) condensed cream-of-chicken soup
> 1 can (10¾ ounces) condensed tomato soup
> 1 can (10¾ ounces) condensed consommé
> 1 tablespoon grated onion
> ¼ teaspoon nutmeg
> 1 cup light cream
> 1 can (6 ounces) lobster, drained, flaked or ⅔ cup fresh
>   lobster meat
> ¼ cup dry sherry

AT SERVING TIME:
> Combine soups with onion, nutmeg and cream in blazer pan over moderate heat. Stir until mixture is heated. Place over boiling water in pan and stir in lobster and sherry. Heat, stirring occasionally.

> *Makes 4 servings.*

TIPS: Lobster Soup served with toasted hard rolls, mixed green salad and fresh fruit and cheese will make a tasty light supper.

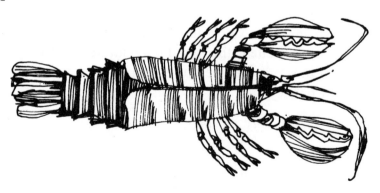

CHEESE AND SHRIMP ALEXANDRIA

ASSEMBLE INGREDIENTS:
  3 tablespoons butter
  3 tablespoons chopped green pepper
  2 tablespoons chopped onion
  2 tablespoons flour
  ½ teaspoon salt
  ½ teaspoon sugar
  Dash Tabasco
  1 cup canned tomatoes
  1½ cups shredded sharp Cheddar cheese
  1 egg, beaten slightly
  ¼ cup undiluted evaporated milk
  1 cup cooked shrimp
  Hot cooked rice

AT SERVING TIME:

Heat butter in blazer pan over moderate heat. Add green pepper and onion and cook a few minutes. Stir in flour and let bubble. Add seasonings and place over boiling water in pan. Slowly stir in tomatoes and cook, stirring occasionally until mixture thickens. Add cheese and stir until cheese melts. Mix egg with evaporated milk and stir into cheese mixture. Continue cooking for a few minutes longer. Add shrimp. When hot, serve over rice.

Makes 4 servings.

TIPS: Cheese and Shrimp Alexandria can be served with broiled peach halves, buttered green beans and spinach salad. Finish with Viennese coffee and cookies.

SHRIMP IN BUTTER SAUCE

ASSEMBLE INGREDIENTS:

½ cup butter
½ clove garlic, mashed
3 cups cleaned, cooked shrimp
2 tablespoons lemon juice
1 tablespoon finely chopped parsley
½ teaspoon salt
Freshly ground pepper to taste

AT SERVING TIME:

Heat butter in blazer pan over moderate heat. Add garlic and shrimp and cook and stir until shrimp is heated through. Place over boiling water in pan and add remaining ingredients. Let flavors blend a few minutes.

Makes 4 servings.

TIPS: With Shrimp in Butter Sauce, serve rice cooked in bouillon, broccoli, fresh-vegetable relishes, blueberry pie and coffee.

SHRIMP PARADISO

ASSEMBLE INGREDIENTS:

3 cups cooked, shelled shrimp
¼ cup butter
½ cup chopped onion
½ cup chopped cucumber
1 clove garlic, chopped
2 cups dairy sour cream
2 teaspoons lemon juice
1 tablespoon chopped chutney
2 teaspoons curry powder
½ teaspoon salt
½ teaspoon ginger
Hot cooked rice

IN ADVANCE:

Devein and wash shrimp. Drain and dry well.

AT SERVING TIME:

Heat butter in blazer pan over moderate heat. Add onion, cucumber and garlic and cook until tender, but not browned. Place over boiling water in pan. Stir in sour cream, lemon juice, chutney, curry powder, salt, ginger and shrimp. Heat, stirring occasionally until mixture is thoroughly heated. Serve over cooked rice.

Makes 4 servings.

TIPS: With Shrimp Paradiso, serve chopped cashews, chutney, toasted coconut, broccoli, tomato slices with fresh herbs in oil and vinegar, and cubed watermelon in mint-flavored gin.

LOBSTER NEWBURG

ASSEMBLE INGREDIENTS:

6 tablespoons butter
2 cups coarsely cut lobster meat
2 tablespoons flour
½ cup dry sherry
4 egg yolks
2 cups thin cream
Salt to taste
Dash Tabasco
⅛ teaspoon nutmeg
4 patty shells or 4 pieces toast

AT SERVING TIME:

Heat butter in blazer pan over moderate heat and cook lobster for 3 minutes. Sprinkle with flour and cook 1 minute longer. Place over hot water in pan and add sherry and cook until hot. Mix egg yolks with cream and add slowly to lobster, stirring constantly. Continue to cook and stir until mixture thickens. Add seasonings. Serve in patty shells or over toast.

Makes 4 servings.

TIPS: Lobster Newburg is an aristocratic dish and deserves an appropriate menu. Serve tiny peas with water chestnuts, a salad of watercress and Boston lettuce with thin sliccs of peeled orange, and hot rolls. For dessert, a meringue with raspberry ice. Demitasse.

SCALLOPS PAULINE

ASSEMBLE INGREDIENTS:
 1 pound scallops
 3 tablespoons butter
 ¼ cup chopped onions
 ½ cup sliced mushrooms
 1 tablespoon flour
 ½ teaspoon salt
 Dash freshly ground pepper
 ½ cup dry white wine
 1 tablespoon lemon juice
 1 tablespoon chopped parsley
 4 pieces toast

IN ADVANCE:
 Wash scallops. If large-sized, cut in quarters. Drain on paper towels.

AT SERVING TIME:

Heat butter in blazer pan over moderate heat. Cook onions and mushrooms in butter for 3 minutes. Stir in flour, salt and pepper and let mixture bubble. Stir in wine and cook and stir until mixture boils and is thickened. Add scallops, lemon juice and parsley and cook 1 minute. Set pan over hot water in water pan to keep hot. Serve on toast.

Makes 4 servings.

TIPS: Scallops Pauline on toast can be the headliner for a meal that also includes buttered asparagus tips, hot rolls, lettuce with Russian dressing, éclairs, and hot tea.

CREAMED CLAMS

ASSEMBLE INGREDIENTS:

2 cans (7 ounces each) minced clams
1½ cups milk and clam juice
4 tablespoons butter
¾ cup finely chopped celery
4 tablespoons flour
½ teaspoon salt
Dash Tabasco
1 tablespoon finely chopped parsley
4 pieces toast

IN ADVANCE:

Drain clams. Measure juice and add milk to make 1½ cups.

AT SERVING TIME:

Heat butter in blazer pan over moderate heat, add celery and cook until tender. Stir in flour and let bubble. Place over boiling water in pan and slowly stir in milk and clam juice. Cook until thickened, stirring occasionally. Add clams, seasonings and parsley. Heat. Serve over toast.

Makes 4 servings.

TIPS: Creamed Clams make a good midnight-supper dish. They go well with beer or ale, and hot French bread and crisp pickles. Have a big bowl of fresh fruit to eat out of hand.

CRAB MEAT BÉCHAMEL

ASSEMBLE INGREDIENTS:

1 can (10½ ounces) chicken broth
1 small onion, sliced
⅛ teaspoon thyme
Dash nutmeg
¼ cup butter
¼ cup flour
½ cup milk
½ cup cream
2 egg yolks, slightly beaten
1 can (13 ounces) crab meat (2 cups cooked)
Dash Tabasco
Salt and freshly ground pepper to taste
4 patty shells

IN ADVANCE:

In a saucepan, combine chicken broth with onion, thyme

and nutmeg and simmer for 15 minutes. Strain. If necessary, add water to make 1 cup.

AT SERVING TIME:

Heat butter in blazer pan over moderate heat. Add the flour and let bubble. Place over hot water in pan and stir in milk and chicken broth. Let cook, stirring occasionally until mixture thickens. Mix cream with egg yolks and stir into hot mixture. Cook and stir until mixture thickens. Add crab meat and season to taste. Reheat. Serve in patty shells.

Makes 4 servings.

TIPS: With Crab Meat Béchamel, one might serve julienne carrots, tomato wedges with crisp lettuce and breadsticks, and melon for dessert.

QUICK SEAFOOD CURRY

ASSEMBLE INGREDIENTS:

2 tablespoons butter
2 to 4 teaspoons curry powder
½ cup onion
2 cans (10 ounces each) frozen condensed cream-of-shrimp soup, thawed
⅔ to 1 cup milk
2 cups flaked cooked crab, lobster or diced cooked shrimp
Hot cooked rice

AT SERVING TIME:

Heat butter in blazer pan over moderate heat. Add curry

powder and onion, cooking onion until tender. Add soup, milk and seafood and place over boiling water in pan. Heat until soup is hot and flavors are blended, stirring often. Serve over rice.

Makes 4 servings.

TIPS: In the Far East, where curries originated, a curry supper was classified by the number of "boys" (servants) it took to carry the accompanying condiments to the table. Make this a "three-boy" curry by serving chopped peanuts, toasted coconut and chutney with it; also, green beans and sliced celery cooked together, and a tossed salad. Have chilled peaches in port wine and hot tea for dessert.

SEAFOOD BARANOFF

ASSEMBLE INGREDIENTS:
>   1 can (4½ ounces) shrimp
>   1 can (13 ounces) crabmeat or fresh shrimp and crab-
>   meat
>   2 tablespoons lemon juice
>   4 tablespoons butter
>   4 tablespoons flour
>   ¼ teaspoon salt
>   1¾ cups milk
>   ½ cup mayonnaise
>   2 tablespoons chopped parsley
>   3 tablespoons chopped pimiento
>   Hot cooked noodles

IN ADVANCE:

Drain shrimp and cut into small pieces. Drain crabmeat and remove cartilage. Mix shrimp and crab with lemon juice.

AT SERVING TIME:

Heat butter in blazer pan over moderate heat. Add flour and salt and cook until bubbly. Stir in milk and cook and stir until mixture boils and is thickened. Place over hot water in pan. Slowly stir in mayonnaise. Add seafood, parsley and pimiento. Cook until hot, stirring occasionally. Serve over noodles.

Makes 4 servings.

TIPS: With Seafood Baranoff, serve buttered carrots, chilled pears with French dressing, cheese cake, and coffee.

OYSTERS-HAM RICHMOND

ASSEMBLE INGREDIENTS:

2 cups cooked, diced ham
1½ cups fresh tomatoes, peeled, diced
¼ cup chopped green onion
¼ cup chopped green pepper
1 cup cooked green lima beans, drained
1 cup whole kernel corn, drained
¼ teaspoon salt
12 large raw oysters, drained
3 tablespoons butter
Salt and freshly ground pepper to taste
4 corn muffins, split and toasted

IN ADVANCE:

Combine ham with tomatoes, onion, green pepper, lima beans, corn and salt in a bowl. Mix lightly. Drain oysters and arrange on plate.

AT SERVING TIME:

Heat butter in blazer pan over moderate heat. Add ham mixture and cook several minutes until heated through. Season to taste with salt and pepper. Place oysters on top of hot mixture. Cover and cook 5 minutes. Serve on toasted corn muffins.

Makes 4 servings.

TIPS: With Oysters-Ham Richmond, the accompanying menu might be apricot and cottage-cheese salad on lettuce; and for dessert, vanilla ice cream with crème de menthe, and coffee.

TUNA SCRAMBLE

ASSEMBLE INGREDIENTS:

    ¼ cup olive oil
    ¼ cup chopped green pepper
    2 cans (6½ or 7 ounces each) tuna, drained (or 2 cups
        flaked cooked fish)
    1 cup cooked rice
    4 hard cooked eggs, chopped
    2 tablespoons soy sauce
    ½ teaspoon salt
    Freshly ground pepper to taste

AT SERVING TIME:

Heat oil in blazer pan over moderate heat. Add green pepper and cook until tender. Add remaining ingredients and stir over moderate heat until thoroughly heated, about 5 minutes. Place over boiling water in pan to keep hot until served.

Makes 4 servings.

TIPS: With Tuna Scramble, a big bowl of stewed tomatoes gently simmered with chopped onions and a nip of sugar, crisp celery sticks and sesame-seed rolls. For dessert, chocolate cake with vanilla ice cream.

CREAMED FINNAN HADDIE

ASSEMBLE INGREDIENTS:
  1½ pounds finnan haddie
  4 tablespoons butter
  4 tablespoons flour
  2 cups milk
  Salt to taste
  ¼ teaspoon freshly ground pepper
  4 pieces toast
  2 tablespoons chopped parsley

IN ADVANCE:
  Cover the finnan haddie with cold water and bring to just below the boiling point. Poach until fish can be flaked easily (about 5 minutes). Drain and flake.

AT SERVING TIME:
  In blazer pan over moderate heat, melt the butter. Add the flour and let bubble. Place over boiling water in pan and stir in the milk. Let cook, stirring occasionally until mixture is thickened. Add salt to taste and pepper and cooked finnan haddie. Heat. Serve over toast and sprinkle chopped parsley over each serving.

  Makes 4 servings.

TIPS: Creamed Finnan Haddie is greatly favored as a brunch

dish. Start the meal with a glass of orange juice and serve hot popovers and strawberry jam with the finnan haddie; also, lots of hot coffee or tea.

CHICKEN VALENCIA

ASSEMBLE INGREDIENTS:

    2 tablespoons butter
    ½ cup chopped green pepper
    ½ cup chopped onion
    ½ cup chopped celery
    1 can (10¾ ounces) cream of mushroom soup
    1 cup chopped mushrooms
    ½ cup chopped stuffed olives
    1 cup chopped cooked chicken
    ½ cup chicken broth
    ½ cup dry white wine
    Salt and freshly ground pepper to taste
    4 pieces toast

AT SERVING TIME:

Heat butter in blazer pan over moderate heat. Add pepper, onion and celery and sauté until tender. Stir in remaining ingredients except toast. Season to taste. Place over boiling water in water pan and let cook until thoroughly heated. Serve on toast.

Makes 4 servings.

TIPS: With Chicken Valencia, pickled peaches, petit pois cooked with shredded lettuce, hot crescent rolls, lemon pudding and tea.

CHICKEN CRÊPES

ASSEMBLE INGREDIENTS:

1 recipe crêpes (page 119)
½ cup butter
½ cup flour
1½ cups light cream
1 cup well-seasoned chicken broth
Salt and freshly ground pepper to taste
2 cups finely chopped cooked chicken
½ cup chopped mushrooms
2 tablespoons dry sherry
2 tablespoons butter
½ cup dairy sour cream

IN ADVANCE:

Prepare 1 recipe crêpes. Cool. Heat butter and flour together until bubbly. Stir in cream and chicken broth and cook and stir until mixture boils and is thickened. Season to taste. Divide sauce into two equal parts. Into one part stir chicken, mushrooms and sherry. Cool. Put a spoonful of this filling on center of each crêpe, dividing equally between crêpes. Roll crêpe around filling.

AT SERVING TIME:

Heat 2 tablespoons butter in blazer pan set over boiling water in pan. Arrange filled crêpes in pan. Mix remainder of sauce with sour cream. Spoon over crêpes in pan. Heat until crêpes and sauce are thoroughly hot.

Makes 4 servings.

TIPS: All of the real work for Chicken Crêpes can be done in advance. Serve it with Belgian canned carrots, watercress salad, and lemon sherbet with raspberries.

CREAMED CHICKEN ORANJESTAD

ASSEMBLE INGREDIENTS:
   3 tablespoons butter
   1 cup sliced fresh mushrooms
   ¼ cup finely chopped onions
   4 tablespoons flour
   1½ cups milk
   2 cups diced cooked chicken
   Salt and freshly ground pepper to taste
   ¼ cup Curacao liqueur
   2 tablespoons chopped parsley
   2 tablespoons chopped pimiento
   4 patty shells or 4 pieces toast

AT SERVING TIME:
   Heat butter in blazer pan over medium heat and cook
   mushrooms and onions until tender, stirring often. Add
   flour and let bubble. Place over boiling water in pan and
   slowly stir in milk. Cook and stir until mixture is thickened. Add chicken and season to taste. When hot, add
   Curacao, parsley and pimiento. Serve in patty shells or
   on toast.

   Makes 4 servings.

TIPS: With Creamed Chicken Oranjestad, one can serve buttered broccoli spears, tiny new potatoes, cucumber salad and
a fruit dessert.

CURRIED CHICKEN BREASTS

ASSEMBLE INGREDIENTS:
   3 whole broiler-fryer chicken breasts
   4 tablespoons butter
   1 small onion, chopped
   1 small apple, pared, cored and chopped
   2 tablespoons flour
   1 teaspoon salt
   1 teaspoon curry powder
   ¼ teaspoon ginger
   1 chicken bouillon cube dissolved in 1 cup boiling water
   ½ cup light cream
   Hot cooked rice

IN ADVANCE:
   Bone chicken and remove skin. Cut each breast half into 10 or 12 strips.

AT SERVING TIME:
   Heat butter in blazer pan over moderate to high heat. Add chicken, onion and apple. Cook, stirring constantly 5 minutes. Sprinkle with flour, salt, curry powder and ginger and stir until flour is moistened. Add bouillon and cream and mix well. Cover and place over boiling water in water pan. Cook, stirring occasionally until mixture is thickened (about 5 minutes longer). Serve over rice.

   Makes 4 servings.

TIPS: Curried Chicken Breasts can also be served with chopped peanuts, toasted coconut, and chutney. You might also add chilled mandarin sections, raisins and grated fresh cucumbers. Have asparagus vinaigrette salad, and butter-pecan ice cream for dessert.

CHICKEN LIVERS SUPERB

ASSEMBLE INGREDIENTS:
⅓ cup butter
1 pound chicken livers, cut in half
¼ cup finely chopped onion
1 teaspoon salt
Freshly ground pepper to taste
1 cup sliced fresh mushrooms
1 tablespoon flour
1 cup half-and-half (or light cream)
2 tablespoons brandy
4 patty shells or 4 pieces toast
4 crisp bacon curls

AT SERVING TIME:
Heat butter in blazer pan over moderate heat. Add chicken livers, onion, salt and pepper. Sauté slowly until chicken livers are just cooked through (about 10 minutes). Add mushrooms during last half of cooking time. Sprinkle flour over chicken livers and place over boiling water in pan. Slowly add half-and-half, stirring carefully. Cook until sauce is thickened. Stir in brandy. Serve in patty shells or on toast. Garnish with bacon curls.

Makes 4 servings.

TIPS: Another excellent brunch dish. With it might be served avocado and grapefruit salad, hot pecan rolls and coffee.

SALMIS OF DUCK

ASSEMBLE INGREDIENTS:

2 tablespoons butter
2 green onions, finely chopped
½ cup pitted ripe olives, sliced
½ cup dry sherry
1 tablespoon lemon juice
1 cup duck gravy
⅛ teaspoon rosemary
⅛ teaspoon thyme
Salt and freshly ground pepper to taste
Sliced cold roast duck for four servings
4 pieces toast

AT SERVING TIME:

Heat butter in blazer pan over medium heat. Sauté onions until tender. Add olives, sherry, lemon juice, gravy and seasonings and stir until mixture is hot. Add duck slices and heat gently for several minutes. Serve at once on toast or keep hot over water pan until ready to serve.

Makes 4 servings.

TIPS: Salmis is a traditional chafing-dish recipe and is always made with wholly or partially cooked game. Serve buttered broccoli, a tossed salad with artichoke hearts, toasted bread and chilled melon.

TURKEY AND VEGETABLES

ASSEMBLE INGREDIENTS:

¼ cup butter
¼ cup flour
1 cup undiluted evaporated milk
1 cup turkey or chicken broth
2 cups diced cooked turkey
¼ cup dry sherry
1 package (10 ounces) mixed frozen vegetables, cooked and drained
⅛ teaspoon nutmeg
Salt and freshly ground pepper to taste
Hot cooked noodles

AT SERVING TIME:

Heat butter in blazer pan over medium heat. Add flour and let bubble. Place over boiling water in pan and gradually stir in milk and broth. Cook and stir until mixture thickens. Add remaining ingredients and heat to serving temperature. Serve over noodles.

Makes 4 servings.

TIPS: Turkey and Vegetables goes nicely with cranberry sauce, a tossed salad and hot rolls. Serve apples and your favorite cheese for dessert along with hot tea.

BEEF STROGANOFF

ASSEMBLE INGREDIENTS:

1½ pounds beef sirloin
2 tablespoons flour
1 teaspoon salt
3 tablespoons butter
¼ cup finely chopped onion
½ pound fresh mushrooms, diced
1 clove garlic, finely chopped
2 tablespoons flour
1 cup beef bouillon
1 tablespoon Worcestershire sauce
1 cup dairy sour cream
Hot cooked noodles

IN ADVANCE:

Remove fat from beef and cut into thin strips about 1½
inches wide and 2 inches long. Dredge with 2 tablespoons
flour and salt.

AT SERVING TIME:

Heat butter in blazer pan over high heat and quickly
brown onions, mushrooms and garlic. Add meat and
brown. Sprinkle remaining 2 tablespoons flour over meat
mixture in pan. Add bouillon and Worcestershire sauce.
Cook and stir until mixture boils and is thickened. Place
over hot water in pan. Stir in sour cream and heat for a
few minutes. Keep over hot (not boiling) water until
ready to serve. Serve over noodles.

Makes 4 servings.

TIPS: With Beef Stroganoff, serve thick slices of broiled tomatoes, crusty French bread, a salad of julienne beets with grated hard-cooked egg and French dressing, a cordial and black coffee for dessert.

BEEF WITH SOUR CREAM

ASSEMBLE INGREDIENTS:

  1 tablespoon butter or margarine
  1 pound ground beef round
  ½ teaspoon salt
  Dash Tabasco
  1 can (2½ to 3 ounces) sliced mushrooms and liquid
  ½ cup bouillon
  2 cups dairy sour cream
  1 can (3½ ounces) French-fried onions
  2 tablespoons chopped parsley
  Hot cooked noodles

AT SERVING TIME:

Heat butter in the blazer pan over high heat. Crumble beef into small pieces and sauté quickly to brown. Add salt, Tabasco, mushrooms and liquid and bouillon and bring to a boil. Place over hot water in pan. Stir in sour cream, onions and parsley. Reheat but do not boil. Serve over noodles.

Makes 4 servings.

TIPS: Serve hot rolls and a tomato aspic liberally laced with chopped celery along with Beef with Sour Cream. A dessert made of sponge cake with blueberries and soft ice cream spooned over it and coffee will top off the meal nicely.

HAM AND EGGS IN MUSTARD SAUCE

ASSEMBLE INGREDIENTS:

¼ cup butter
¼ cup flour
½ teaspoon dry mustard
2 cups milk
1½ cups diced cooked ham
4 hard-cooked eggs
Salt and freshly ground pepper to taste
2 tablespoons chopped parsley
Hot waffle sections

AT SERVING TIME:

Heat butter in blazer pan over moderate heat. Add flour and mustard and cook until mixture bubbles. Place over boiling water in pan and gradually stir in milk. Cook and stir until mixture is smooth and thickened. Add diced ham and hard-cooked eggs cut in eighths and season to taste. Keep hot until ready to serve. Sprinkle with chopped parsley. Serve over waffle sections.

Makes 4 servings.

TIPS: Served over hot waffle sections (made to order or toaster-heated frozen), Ham and Eggs in Mustard Sauce makes an ideal brunch or late-supper dish. With this dish, serve green-beans vinaigrette and a chilled fruit cup of mixed fresh fruit with cranberry-sherbet topping.

MEATBALLS PIEMONTE

ASSEMBLE INGREDIENTS:

Meatballs:

1½ pounds ground beef chuck

½ clove garlic, crushed

¼ cup chopped onion

¼ teaspoon oregano

1½ teaspoons salt

¾ cup breadcrumbs

2 teaspoons prepared mustard

Dash Tabasco

1½ teaspoons Worcestershire sauce

Flour

Sauce:

4 strips bacon, cut into small pieces

¾ cup strong coffee

½ cup Burgundy wine

¼ cup water

¾ teaspoon salt

¾ teaspoon sugar

1 tablespoon flour

¾ cup dairy sour cream

Hot cooked noodles

IN ADVANCE:

Mix ground beef with remaining ingredients except flour and form into about 16 meatballs. Dust with flour.

AT SERVING TIME:

Cook bacon in blazer pan over moderate heat until crisp. Remove from pan and brown meatballs on all sides. Add coffee, wine, water, salt and sugar and bring to a boil. Place over boiling water in pan and cover and cook 15 minutes. Return bacon to pan. Mix flour with a little water and stir into mixture. Cook until thickened. When ready to serve, garnish mixture with spoons of sour cream. Serve with noodles.

Makes 4 servings.

TIPS: This is a hearty main dish, and a simple watercress-and-lettuce salad, crusty buttered bread, and sherbet for dessert should do.

SWEETBREADS WITH BACON

ASSEMBLE INGREDIENTS:
    2 pairs sweetbreads
    Cold water
    Lemon juice (or vinegar)
    1 egg, beaten
    2 tablespoons milk
    ¼ teaspoon salt
    Freshly ground pepper
    ½ cup (approximately) dried breadcrumbs
    8 slices bacon

IN ADVANCE:
    Soak sweetbreads in cold water for at least 1 hour. Simmer for 15 minutes in fresh water to which 1 tablespoon lemon juice or 1 teaspoon vinegar per quart of water has been added. Drain at once and cool. Remove membrane. Cut in ¼-inch-thick slices. Mix egg with milk, salt, and pepper. Dip sweetbread slices in breadcrumbs, then in egg mixture, and again in crumbs. Arrange on plate ready to cook.

AT SERVING TIME:

In blazer pan over moderate heat, fry bacon until crisp. Remove and keep warm. Sauté crumbed sweetbread slices until lightly browned on each side. Serve with bacon.

Makes 4 servings.

TIPS: With Sweetbreads with Bacon, creamed potatoes and peas, hard rolls, cucumber-and-lettuce salad and half cantaloupe and coffee could be your choice.

STEAK DIANE

ASSEMBLE INGREDIENTS:

1 pound boneless sirloin steak
2 tablespoons butter
2 teaspoons olive oil
½ teaspoon dry mustard
1 teaspoon chopped chives
Salt
Freshly ground pepper
1 teaspoon chopped parsley
1 teaspoon Worcestershire sauce
1 tablespoon lemon juice

IN ADVANCE:

Trim all fat from steak and cut into 2 or 3 serving portions. With a mallet, pound very thin.

AT SERVING TIME:

Heat 1 tablespoon butter and 1 teaspoon olive oil in blazer pan over moderate heat. Add mustard and chives.

Brush steak with remaining oil and season with salt and pepper to taste. Quickly brown on both sides, about 1½ minutes. Remove steak to warm platter. Add parsley, Worcestershire sauce, lemon juice and remaining butter to blazer pan. Blend quickly and pour over steak.

Makes 2 to 3 servings.

TIPS: With Steak Diane one might serve baked stuffed potatoes, macédoine of vegetable salad, and vanilla soufflé.

VEAL SAGAMORE

ASSEMBLE INGREDIENTS:
    2 tablespoons butter
    ½ clove garlic, finely chopped
    2 tablespoons finely chopped onion
    1½ tablespoons flour
    1 cup well-flavored chicken broth
    Salt and freshly ground pepper to taste
    4 tablespoons currant jelly
    ½ teaspoon rosemary
    6 to 8 thin slices cold roast veal

AT SERVING TIME:
    Heat butter in blazer pan over moderate heat. Add garlic and onion and cook 3 minutes. Stir in flour and let bubble. Stir in chicken broth and cook and stir until mixture boils and is thickened. Season to taste with salt and pepper. Mix in currant jelly and rosemary. Place over boiling water in pan and carefully put veal slices in sauce. Cook until veal is thoroughly heated.

Makes 4 servings.

TIPS: With Veal Sagamore, serve hot buttered noodles, Brussels sprouts, tomato cottage-cheese salad, fresh blueberries (in season) and cream.

VEAL KIDNEYS CLEMENTINE

ASSEMBLE INGREDIENTS:
   3 veal kidneys
   4 tablespoons butter
   2 cloves garlic, finely minced
   3 tablespoons flour
   1 teaspoon salt
   Freshly ground pepper to taste
   1½ cups Burgundy wine
   Hot cooked rice

IN ADVANCE:
   Remove fat from veal kidneys and slice into thin slices.

AT SERVING TIME:
   Heat butter in blazer pan over moderate heat and sauté kidneys and garlic until lightly browned. Sprinkle flour, salt and pepper over kidneys and stir until flour mixture bubbles. Slowly stir in wine. Cook 5 minutes. Serve with rice at once or keep hot over water pan.

   Makes 4 servings.

TIPS: This quickly prepared dish goes well with buttered peas and mushrooms, lettuce wedges with Roquefort dressing, stewed pears and macaroons.

NOODLES ALFREDO

ASSEMBLE INGREDIENTS:

    1 package (8 ounces) medium egg noodles
    ½ cup butter, cut in pieces
    Freshly ground pepper to taste
    ⅔ cup light cream
    4 ounces grated Parmesan cheese

IN ADVANCE:

Cook noodles in boiling salted water, slightly *al dente*. Drain. Keep warm.

AT SERVING TIME:

Place hot noodles in blazer pan over moderate heat. Add butter and pepper to taste and toss gently with a fork while butter melts. Add cream and continue tossing until cream is absorbed. Sprinkle the Parmesan cheese over the noodles and continue tossing gently until all noodles are coated with cheese and cheese is melted. Serve at once.

Makes 2 to 3 servings.

TIPS: With Noodles Alfredo, serve buttered asparagus, tossed salad, Italian breadsticks, fresh strawberries with kirsch, and coffee.

SCRAMBLED EGGS

ASSEMBLE INGREDIENTS:

    8 eggs
    ⅓ cup water
    ½ teaspoon salt
    Freshly ground pepper to taste
    3 tablespoons butter

IN ADVANCE:

Beat eggs with water and salt and pepper until just mixed.

AT SERVING TIME:

Heat butter in blazer pan over moderate heat until melted. Place over hot water in water pan. Pour egg mixture into butter and cook, stirring from bottom, until eggs are thick and creamy. Serve at once.

Makes 4 servings.

VARIATIONS:

1. Add 2 tablespoons each chopped parsley and chives to egg mixture. Sprinkle additional chopped parsley on cooked eggs.
2. Sauté 1 cup sliced fresh mushrooms in butter before adding eggs. Add ¼ teaspoon garlic salt.
3. Add ¾ cup creamy cottage cheese to egg mixture. Add ½ teaspoon seasoned salt.
4. Sauté 6 cherry tomatoes and 1 chopped green onion in butter before adding eggs.
5. Fold ½ cup grated sharp Cheddar cheese into egg mixture.

TIPS: Serve Scrambled Eggs, plain or varied, with sautéed slices of ham, hot biscuits, and preserves. Serve for supper, brunch, or breakfast.

SHRIMP AND EGGS

ASSEMBLE INGREDIENTS:
- ½ pound frozen cooked, shelled and deveined shrimp
- 3 slices bacon
- 6 eggs, beaten
- ¼ cup light cream
- ½ teaspoon Worcestershire sauce
- ½ cup chopped onion
- ¾ cup chopped green pepper
- ½ teaspoon salt
- ¼ teaspoon cayenne pepper

IN ADVANCE:

Defrost shrimp. Cook bacon until crisp. Reserve 2 table-spoons bacon fat. Crumble bacon and mix with eggs, cream and Worcestershire sauce in a bowl.

AT SERVING TIME:

Put reserved bacon fat in blazer pan over moderate heat. Add onion and green pepper and sauté until tender but not browned. Add shrimp, salt and cayenne and stir until shrimp is hot. Place over boiling water in water pan and add egg mixture. Cook and stir until mixture thickens and eggs are firm.

Makes 4 to 6 servings.

TIPS: Shrimp and Eggs makes a standout brunch main dish. Chilled orange and cranberry juice might be served first, with broiled peaches, celery and olives and hot brioche.

EGGS DORADO

ASSEMBLE INGREDIENTS:
  1 can (1 pound) tomatoes
  1¼ teaspoon chili powder
  ¼ pound shredded American process cheese
  6 eggs, beaten
  2 tablespoons bacon fat
  ¼ pound cut-up dried beef
  4 hard rolls, split and toasted

IN ADVANCE:
  In a bowl, mix tomatoes with chili powder, cheese and eggs.

AT SERVING TIME:
  Heat fat in blazer pan over moderate heat. Add dried beef and cook until frizzled, 2 to 3 minutes. Place over boiling water in water pan and stir in tomato mixture. Cook and stir until mixture is thickened. Serve over toasted rolls.

  Makes 4 servings.

DESSERTS IN
THE CHAFING DISH

As all good cooks know, a spectacular dessert will rescue an otherwise so-so meal. And certainly the two most famous chafing-dish desserts. Crêpes Suzette and Cherries Jubilee, are spectacular enough to give blessings even to coldcuts. But one doesn't have to stop with these two examples. There are a number of other desserts that adapt themselves to chafing-dish treatment. One can also use the chafing dish as a serving piece for a variety of hot ice-cream sauces that are not necessarily cooked in the dish.

In setting up for flaming (flambéed) desserts, it is wise to practice before strutting at the table. Three hints: 1. Always warm the liquor to be flamed. 2. Use long fireplace matches for the crucial moment of igniting the liquor. They are more graceful-looking and enable the table chef to escape any sudden blaze. 3. If you have trouble igniting food, put part of the warm liquor or liqueur in a ladle, the remainder in the dish to be blazed. Light the liquor in the ladle and pour blazing into the food. As a matter of safety, never pour liquor directly from the bottle onto any blazing foods. Use a small pitcher or other suitable container.

Many flaming desserts are really a type of sauce to be served over ice cream. To do this gracefully, dish the ice cream in serving-size scoops and pile lightly into a handsome bowl. Store in the freezer and bring to the table when ready to serve with the hot sauce. This makes it easier for the person serving. When a dessert is in two parts like this, it is perfectly permissible (in fact preferable) for the person on the right of the chef to put the ice cream into individual dishes and hand them to the chef to spoon over the sauce. This makes for neater and faster service.

CHERRIES JUBILEE

ASSEMBLE INGREDIENTS:

2 cans (1 pound each) pitted dark, sweet cherries
¼ cup sugar
1 teaspoon cornstarch
¼ cup warm kirsch (or Cointreau)
1 quart vanilla ice cream

IN ADVANCE:

Drain juice from cherries. Save juice and put cherries in a container.

AT SERVING TIME:

Put 1 cup cherry juice in blazer pan over moderate heat. Add sugar mixed with cornstarch and cook and stir until mixture boils and is thickened. Add cherries and cook until cherries are heated. Place over boiling water in water pan. Pour kirsch or Cointreau over cherries and sauce and ignite. Serve the flaming sauce over ice cream.

Makes 8 servings.

BASIC CRÊPES RECIPE

ASSEMBLE INGREDIENTS:
½ cup sifted flour
1 egg
1 egg yolk
⅛ teaspoon salt
1 teaspoon sugar
1 cup milk
2 tablespoons butter, melted and cooled

IN ADVANCE:
Put sifted flour into bowl. Add remaining ingredients and beat with wire whisk or rotary eggbeater until very smooth. Chill for two hours or longer. Grease a 6- or 7-inch skillet and heat over moderate heat. Pour about 2 tablespoons batter into skillet to form a paper thin layer. Brown on both sides. Remove from skillet and cool on cake rack. Make 16 crêpes in this manner. Fold into quarters or thirds.

Makes 16 crêpes.

TIPS:
1. Stir batter each time before putting into skillet.
2. Pour batter into center of skillet. Lift skillet to spread batter evenly over bottom surface.
3. When crêpe begins to look dry on surface and bubbles form in center, it is ready to turn.

CRÊPES SUZETTE

ASSEMBLE INGREDIENTS:
- ¼ cup butter
- ¾ cup sugar
- ½ cup orange juice
- 1 teaspoon orange rind
- ½ cup Cointreau (or curaçao)
- ½ cup warm brandy

IN ADVANCE:

Prepare 16 crêpes (see previous recipe).

AT SERVING TIME:

Heat butter in blazer pan over moderate heat. Add sugar, orange juice, rind, and Cointreau or curaçao. Cook and stir until mixture boils. Place over boiling water in water pan and add the folded crêpes. Spoon sauce over crêpes until thoroughly heated. Pour warm brandy over crêpes and sauce in pan and ignite. Serve 4 crêpes and sauce for each serving.

Makes 4 servings.

TIP: Because the crêpes can be made hours or days in advance and frozen, this dessert is not nearly so difficult as it would seem at first glance.

CRÊPES MARGUERITE

ASSEMBLE INGREDIENTS:
  ½ cup butter
  ¼ cup sugar
  1 cup orange juice
  ¼ cup lemon juice
  1 strip lemon rind
  1 strip orange rind
  ½ cup Cointreau
  ½ cup kirsch
  ¼ cup cognac

IN ADVANCE:

  Prepare 16 crêpes (see page 119). Fold in thirds or quarters.

AT SERVING TIME:

  Melt butter in blazer pan over moderate heat. When melted, add sugar, orange juice, lemon juice and rinds. Stir until sugar is dissolved and then add Cointreau and kirsch. When warm, put in folded crêpes and heat and spoon sauce over them until they are heated through. Put cognac in ladle with one cube sugar. Ignite and pour over crêpes and sauce to ignite sauce mixture. Flaming crêpes can be served on plates or flames can be allowed to die down before serving. Serve 4 crêpes with sauce for each serving.

  Makes 4 servings.

HOT PEACH MELBA

ASSEMBLE INGREDIENTS:
  1 package (10 ounces) frozen red raspberries
  4 teaspoons cornstarch
  ¼ cup sugar
  1 tablespoon butter
  8 canned peach halves
  4 scoops vanilla ice cream
  2 tablespoons lemon juice
  ¼ cup ruby port wine

IN ADVANCE:
  Defrost raspberries. Drain juice into pretty container and reserve raspberries in a decorative bowl. Mix raspberry juice with cornstarch, sugar and butter. Arrange peach halves in serving dishes. Arrange ice cream scoops in bowl and store in freezer.

AT SERVING TIME:
  In blazer pan over moderate heat, cook and stir raspbery juice mixture until it boils and is thickened. Stir in lemon juice, wine and raspberries. Cook, stirring lightly until heated through. Serve at once or keep hot over water in pan. To serve, put ice cream into peach halves. Top with raspberry sauce.

  Makes 4 servings.

TIPS: Hot Peach Melba is patterned after the classic peach melba, in which the melba sauce is served chilled. If you have any sauce left over, chill it for future use. Some people might like a crisp sugar wafer served with it.

ORANGE GLAZED BANANAS

ASSEMBLE INGREDIENTS:
    4 large firm bananas
    3 tablespoons butter
    ¾ cup brown sugar, firmly packed
    ¾ cup orange juice
    4 teaspoons grated orange rind
    ¾ teaspoon ginger
    1 quart vanilla ice cream

AT SERVING TIME:
Peel and cut bananas in half lengthwise and then cross-wise. Heat butter in blazer pan over moderate heat and add brown sugar, orange juice, rind and ginger and stir to blend. Heat until bubbly. Add bananas and heat 3 to 5 minutes, stirring and basting. Serve at once or keep hot over water in pan until ready to serve. Then spoon hot bananas into dessert dishes and top with a serving of ice cream.

Makes 8 servings.

ROSY FRUIT FLAMBÉ

ASSEMBLE INGREDIENTS:
    1 can (1 pound 4½ ounces) pineapple chunks
    1 can (1 pound 1 ounce) sliced cling peaches
    3 tablespoons butter
    ½ cup red currant jelly
    1 teaspoon grated lemon rind
    ¾ cup warm wild-cherry brandy
    1 quart vanilla ice cream

IN ADVANCE:

Drain pineapple and peaches. Reserve ¼ cup syrup from pineapple.

AT SERVING TIME:

Melt butter in blazer pan over moderate heat. Add jelly, lemon rind and syrup from pineapple. Stir to blend ingredients. Place over boiling water in water pan and add fruit. Cook and stir until fruit is thoroughly hot. Then add warm wild-cherry brandy. Stir for a few seconds and ignite. To serve, spoon ice cream into serving dishes and top with fruit mixture.

Makes 8 servings.

BANANAS CONNOISSEUR

ASSEMBLE INGREDIENTS:

4 large firm bananas, sliced in 1-inch pieces
2 tablespoons lime juice
¼ cup butter
½ cup sugar
½ cup apricot brandy
1 cup dairy sour cream

AT SERVING TIME:

Sprinkle bananas with lime juice. Heat butter in blazer pan over moderate heat. Add bananas and sauté quickly. Stir in sugar and apricot brandy, stirring until sugar is dissolved. Simmer for 5 minutes. Serve at once or keep hot over water in water pan until ready to serve. Then spoon hot bananas into dessert dishes. Top with sour cream.

Makes 4 servings.

GINGER PEACHY

ASSEMBLE INGREDIENTS:

   1 can (1 pound 13 ounces) peach halves
   ¼ cup sugar
   1 teaspoon cornstarch
   2 tablespoons butter
   ½ cup warm ginger-flavored brandy

AT SERVING TIME:

Drain peaches and put juice into blazer pan over moderate heat. Stir in sugar mixed with cornstarch and cook and stir until mixture boils and is thickened. Add butter and peach halves and place over boiling water in pan. Spoon sauce over peaches until they are thoroughly heated. Pour warm ginger-flavored brandy over peaches and ignite.

Makes 4 servings.

BLAZING BEAUTY

ASSEMBLE INGREDIENTS:

   1 can (1 pound 14 ounces) whole peeled apricots
   ¼ cup butter
   ½ cup apricot jam
   ½ teaspoon cinnamon
   ¼ teaspoon nutmeg
   1 can (1 pound 1 ounce) pitted Bing cherries, drained
   ¾ cup warm wild-cherry–flavored brandy
   1 quart vanilla ice cream

IN ADVANCE:

Drain apricots. Reserve ¼ cup syrup. Remove pits and cut apricots in half.

AT SERVING TIME:

Heat butter in blazer pan over low heat. Add apricot jam, syrup from apricots, and spices. Stir to blend. Place over boiling water in pan. Add fruits and cook and stir until fruit is thoroughly heated. Add warm wild-cherry–flavored brandy. Stir for a few seconds and ignite. To serve, spoon ice cream into serving dishes and top with fruit mixture.

Makes 8 servings.

BURNING APPLES

ASSEMBLE INGREDIENTS:

4 baking apples
½ cup (approximately) moist mincemeat
½ cup brown sugar
2 tablespoons butter
2 tablespoons water

IN ADVANCE:

Core and remove peel from top half of apples. Place in baking dish and fill centers with mincemeat. Sprinkle sugar over apples, dot with butter and pour water in bottom of dish. Bake in moderate oven (375° F.) 30 to 40 minutes or until apples are tender. Do not refrigerate apples.

ASSEMBLE INGREDIENTS:

Sauce:

⅓ cup bourbon

3 tablespoons sugar

2 tablespoons lemon juice

¼ cup warm bourbon

AT SERVING TIME:

Pour any juice from baking apples into blazer pan and add ⅓ cup bourbon, sugar and lemon juice and place over moderate heat. Stir until sugar is dissolved, then add baked apples. Baste apples with liquid and heat until apples are warm. Pour ¼ cup warm bourbon over apples and ignite.

Makes 4 servings.

TIP: If you and your guests don't need to watch calories, serve the apples with a pitcher of cream.

BANANAS FLAMBÉ

ASSEMBLE INGREDIENTS:

4 tablespoons butter

4 bananas, peeled

¼ cup lemon juice

¼ cup sugar

½ cup warm rum

AT SERVING TIME:

Heat butter in blazer pan over moderate heat and sauté bananas (whole or cut in half) until lightly browned.

Add lemon juice and sugar, then heat. Add warm rum and ignite. Serve bananas immediately.

Makes 4 servings.

TIP: When choosing bananas for cooking, pick those which are not too ripe and still slightly green.

Sauces to Serve Warm over Ice Cream

HOT-FUDGE SAUCE

ASSEMBLE INGREDIENTS:
    1 bar (9¾ ounces) milk chocolate
    ½ cup half-and-half (milk and cream)
    3 tablespoons butter
    Dash salt
    1 teaspoon vanilla

IN ADVANCE:
    Break chocolate into small pieces. Combine chocolate, half-and-half, butter and salt in saucepan. Place over very low heat until chocolate is melted. Beat until smooth. Stir in vanilla. Serve warm over ice cream.

Makes 1⅔ cups.

CHERRY-ALMOND SAUCE

ASSEMBLE INGREDIENTS:
    ¼ cup slivered almonds
    2 tablespoons butter
    1 can (1 pound) dark, sweet cherries, pitted
    1½ teaspoons cornstarch
    ¼ teaspoon almond extract

IN ADVANCE:

Sauté almonds in butter until light golden brown. Drain cherry juice into saucepan. Stir in cornstarch and cook and stir over low heat until thickened and clear. Add cherries and almonds. Heat and stir in almond extract. Serve warm over ice cream.

Makes 2 cups.

BUTTERSCOTCH SAUCE

ASSEMBLE INGREDIENTS:

½ cup butter
½ cup light brown sugar, firmly packed
½ cup granulated sugar
⅓ cup whipping cream
¼ cup light corn syrup
Dash salt

IN ADVANCE:

Combine all ingredients. Place over low heat and bring to full boil, stirring until sugar is dissolved. Boil 1 minute. Serve warm over ice cream.

Makes 1½ cups.

CARAMEL-COFFEE SAUCE

ASSEMBLE INGREDIENTS:
   ⅓ cup butter
   1 cup sugar
   1 cup half-and-half (milk and cream)
   1 tablespoon instant coffee
   1 tablespoon cornstarch
   Dash salt

IN ADVANCE:

Melt butter in saucepan. Add sugar and cook and stir over medium heat until sugar dissolves and is caramel color. Combine remaining ingredients and stir into caramel mixture. Continue cooking until sauce is smooth and slightly thickened, stirring. Serve warm over ice cream.

Makes 1¾ cups.

Ice-Cream-Sundae Bar

An ice-cream–sundae bar is great fun for adults as well as for the preteen group. If more than one chafing dish is available, have more than one hot sauce. Otherwise have one hot and several cold. There can also be several kinds of ice cream and a number of things to sprinkle on, over or under the ice cream and sauce. Put out such items as chopped nuts, maraschino cherries, whipped cream, coconut, marshmallow sauce, chocolate sprinkles and bananas for banana splits. Let your imagination take over.

CHAFING-DISH BEVERAGES

There are several beverages that may be prepared in and served from the chafing dish. The best known is Café Brûlot, two versions of which are given below. The one without chocolate is perhaps the classic recipe, but the other is also excellent. There are many variations of Swedish Glögg, and the simple one given here is good and is an appropriate drink at Christmas, the traditional season in which Glögg is served.

To do justice to beverage service from the chafing dish, one should have a handsome ladle for serving and a set of all-purpose cups or mugs and/or demitasse cups. These blazing drinks are particularly interesting to make and to watch while being made as well as being delightful to the taste.

CAFÉ BRÛLOT

ASSEMBLE INGREDIENTS:
- 1 long strip orange peel
- 1 long strip lemon peel
- 3 small cubes sugar
- 1 small stick cinnamon
- 1½ cups cognac
- 2 cups hot demitasse-strength coffee

131

AT SERVING TIME:

Combine the orange and lemon peels with sugar, cinnamon, and cognac in the blazer pan over moderate heat. When warm, place over boiling water in pan. Fill a ladle with additional cognac and a cube of sugar. Ignite and lower into spiced cognac mixture to light. Stir and carefully pour hot coffee into the blazing mixture. When the blaze dies down, serve in Brûlot or demitasse cups.

Makes 6 servings.

TIP: Demitasse-strength coffee is stronger than regular coffee.

CAFÉ BRÛLOT (with chocolate)

ASSEMBLE INGREDIENTS:

1 cup cognac
4 small cinnamon sticks
16 whole cloves
20 small cubes sugar
4 tablespoons chocolate syrup
4 long strips orange peel
4 strips lemon peel
4 cups hot demitasse-strength coffee

AT SERVING TIME:

Put cognac, cinnamon, cloves, sugar, chocolate syrup, orange and lemon peels in blazer pan over moderate heat. When warm, put over hot water in water pan. Fill a ladle with additional cognac and a cube of sugar. Ignite and lower into mixture in blazer pan to light. Stir and carefully pour hot coffee into the blazing mixture and continue stirring. When the blaze dies down, serve in Brûlot or demitasse cups.

Makes about 8 servings.

TIP: Serve small, rich cookies with the Brûlot.

GLÖGG À LA AMERICAN

ASSEMBLE INGREDIENTS:
    2 tablespoons aromatic bitters
    ¾ cup sugar
    2 cups claret
    2 cups dry sherry
    1 cup brandy
    Seeded raisins
    Unsalted almonds

AT SERVING TIME:
Combine bitters with sugar, wines, and brandy in blazer pan over moderate heat. When steaming, place over boiling water in water pan to keep warm. Fill a ladle with additional brandy and a cube of sugar. Ignite and lower into wine-and-brandy mixture. Start serving while still burning. Serve in old-fashioned glasses or demitasse cups with one raisin and one almond in each serving. If you are using old-fashioned glasses, put a spoon in glass when serving hot Glögg to keep glass from breaking.

Makes 12 servings.

CHOCOLATE MONTEZUMA

ASSEMBLE INGREDIENTS:
    ½ cup semisweet chocolate chips
    1 cup sweet sherry wine
    Dash salt
    ¼ teaspoon cinnamon
    3 cups milk, heated
    ½ cup cream, heated
    ½ cup heavy cream, whipped
    Cinnamon

AT SERVING TIME:

Combine chocolate chips, wine, salt and cinnamon in blazer pan. Place over boiling water in water pan and stir until chocolate is melted and blended with wine. Stir in hot milk and cream, blending with a French whisk. When steaming hot, serve in cups with a fluff of whipped cream and a dusting of cinnamon.

Makes 6 servings.

3.
THE CASSEROLE

Originally, the casserole denoted a kind of stew pan—the word being the diminutive of *casse,* French for an "open-mouthed pan of large proportions." The definition has evolved to include both the pan and the food cooked in it.

To the American a casserole is, as a rule, a one-dish meal that is baked in the oven. In Europe a casserole is also a one-dish meal, but it is just as likely to be cooked on top of the range as in the oven.

Technically, a casserole as a food is a recipe that has two or more ingredients, so that, for example, veal with mushrooms baked in a wine sauce is a casserole. On the other hand, if the one-dish-meal concept is accepted, more than two elements should be included. Therefore recipes for both types are included here.

Casseroles have achieved great popularity because they can be prepared in advance, baked in the oven and served in the same dish, freeing the host or hostess for more time with the guests. Because casserole recipes vary from the simple pantry-shelf combinations quickly put together to elaborate dishes, they are equally suitable for family meals or for entertaining on all but the most formal occasions.

136

THE CONTAINER

In cost, casseroles (the containers) range all the way from less than one dollar for a simple 1-quart Pyrex round glass container with cover, to thirty or more times that amount for a large, heavy, enameled cast-iron pot also with cover. Sizes range all the way from 1 pint or less up to 8 and even 12 quarts, with just about every size in-between being available. Shapes range from oval, round, to square, and they may be shallow, deep or in-between. Some have single handles much like a sauce pot, others have two ears to grasp, and some are made without handles of any sort.

If you are going to do any amount of casserole cooking, you will want to have an assortment of sizes, such as a 1½-quart, a 3-quart and a 6-quart to cover all possible occasions from a small family dinner to servings for eight or ten.

The range of materials from which the casseroles are made is also wide. Some of these are decorated in a colorful way and make an attractive appearance on the buffet or dining-room table. Each person will have some preference with regard to physical properties. The following list should be helpful for your selection.

137

Materials

Copper: Pans made of copper are extremely handsome. They come in a variety of sizes, are primarily fairly shallow in depth and can be used top-range, in the oven and under the broiler as well. Copper casseroles need care in polishing and seeing that the inside is kept retinned.

Enameled Steel or Iron: These two materials make popular casseroles because of the myriad possibilities in the colors of the enameled finishes. One can find colors and patterns to suit almost any decorative scheme and to brighten the table. They can be used top-range as well as in the oven.

Aluminum: Casseroles now on the market with this metal as a base are scarcely recognizable as aluminum. They have baked-on enamel finishes outside and nonstick finishes on the inside. The outer finishes enable them to be made in many decorator colors and the inner finish denotes a pan easy to clean. One handsome casserole line being produced even has a ceramic finish on an aluminum base. Most aluminum casseroles can be used top-range and under the broiler as well as in the oven, but check the manufacturers directions to be sure.

Ceramics: Porcelainware is an extremely handsome member of the ceramic family and comes in a variety of shapes and decorations. As a rule, soufflé dishes are made of porcelain. These are straight-sided, generally with a fluted outer surface. They can be purchased as small as ⅓ cup and as large as several quarts. While they are especially designed for soufflés, they can be used for other baking. Do not use this-type casserole top-range unless directions so specify.

Pottery or earthenware is a homey material for casseroles, and many people feel it is the most suitable. Most pottery casseroles are available in a variety of sizes and many can be used top-range, but be sure to check and see that yours is that type.

Pyroceram, a ceramic that is an outgrowth of the space age, is handsome and modern. It comes in a wide range of sizes and can be used top-range and under the broiler as well as in the oven. It can also go directly from freezer to oven.

Glass is the old standby. Clear flameproof glass is available, but many decorator colors and patterns are also on the market. A wide variety of sizes and shapes can be found. To be safe, use it in the oven only, unless there are directions for other uses.

Individual Casseroles: These can be purchased in most of the above materials. One can also find large scallop shapes for use in cooking dishes like Scallops in Wine. Choice of individual pots generally depends on the kind of recipe being prepared. However, a set of shells for seafood preparations and a set of small casserole miniatures would both be useful.

There are also electric casseroles on the market, and many deep electric skillets might come into the European top-range-casserole category.

In planning a casserole-pan wardrobe, take into consideration your uses of the pan. For the average family a complete casserole wardrobe might include the following items: one set of individual casseroles; two in a size for family recipes; a flat casserole for lasagna-type dishes; a large casserole for entertaining; and it is nice to have a soufflé dish. If all other things are equal, when choosing casseroles buy those with lids. It is possible to cover a casserole with aluminum foil, but it is more convenient to have a lid that was made for the pan.

In choosing a casserole, also consider how easy it will be to clean. How easy is it to remove from the oven when full of food? Does it suit the types of recipes most often prepared? And remember that they come to the table, so buy those that can put their best face forward.

THE RECIPE

Because the purpose of this book is to enable you to use and enjoy casserole, chafing-dish and fondue-pot dishes to the fullest, the recipes that can be baked in the casserole are not limited to main dishes. In fact, their use can encompass the whole meal, and many a thrifty homemaker has planned "oven dinners" to make full use of the heat being expended when using the oven for baking.

There are vegetable, potato or other side-dish casseroles that can be served with grilled meats, as well as oven dinners in which the menu might be planned around a meat loaf or pork-chop bake.

Many desserts that have retained their popularity for generations are basically casserole desserts. Such dishes as rice-and-raisin pudding, date-bread pudding, fruit cobblers, and Indian pudding are all baked in casserole pans. The glamorous dessert soufflé is included in this classification. So take advantage of the fact that oven-cooking needs less watching, can encompass get-ready-ahead efficiency, very often takes advantage of less expensive foods and adds variety to your menu-planning.

140

General Tips for Use of the Casserole Pan

1. When a recipe calls for a flat pan it means one from 1½ to 2 inches in depth. A pan too much deeper will change the baking time indicated and may also mean that the finished dish will be of a different texture, since the evaporation will not be the same as in a flat pan.

2. With the exception of soufflés, most pans should be buttered.

3. If casseroles are being specifically prepared for freezing, underbake, as some additional cooking will occur when the casserole is heated at serving time. The most efficient way to bake casseroles for freezing is as follows: Butter the pan and line with heavy (freezer) aluminum foil, using enough foil so that the top of the dish can be covered after baking. Put food in the foil-lined casserole and bake a little less than the time specified in the recipe. Cool. Cover top with the extra foil and freeze. When frozen solid, remove from pan. Overwrap the foil with transparent saran or put into a plastic bag. Seal and date. Return to freezer. If the dish that is frozen is highly spiced, do not plan to keep more than six weeks. Other dishes may be kept as long as six months in a zero-degree freezer. To bake, remove wrappings and place frozen food in original buttered casserole in which it was baked. Cover the top loosely and defrost at room temperature or in the refrigerator. Bake at original temperature until heated through.

4. In choosing a casserole in which to bake a recipe, use a pan that most nearly fits the contents. If the pan is much too large, the food will not brown on the top.

5. If your casserole recipe is a true one-dish meal, you will want to serve only a salad, dessert and coffee. Some recipes are of the two- or three-ingredient type and may call for a side dish of potatoes or rice and a green vegetable as well.

MAIN-COURSE CASSEROLES

Included in this section are casseroles for beef, pork, lamb, veal, chicken, fish and seafoods and cheese. Some are relatively simple to prepare, others take many ingredients and more time. All are worthy of your best efforts. Most can either be prepared in advance ready for cooking, or cooked in advance and reheated at serving time. This is one of the blessings of casserole cookery.

BEEF CHIANTI

2 tablespoons oil
2 cloves garlic, chopped
2 pounds beef cubed for stew
2 tablespoons flour
2 teaspoons salt
¼ teaspoon freshly ground pepper
2 cans (8 ounces each) tomato sauce
2 cups Chianti wine
2 cups water
1 teaspoon oregano
½ teaspoon basil
½ teaspoon thyme
1 teaspoon Worcestershire sauce
2 cloves, crushed
Pinch crushed red pepper
1 bay leaf
8 small white onions, peeled
4 carrots, cut crosswise
4 medium potatoes, cut in large dice

Heat oil in skillet. Add garlic and meat and brown. Sprinkle with flour, salt and pepper. Transfer meat to 3-quart casserole. Add tomato sauce, wine and water to skillet and heat and scrape brown crust from skillet. Add seasonings and pour over beef in casserole. Add vegetables. Cover and bake in a 300° F. oven for 2 hours or until beef is tender.

Makes 4 to 6 servings.

BEEF PONTE VECCHIO

4 slices bacon
2 pounds lean beef, cubed
¼ cup flour
1½ teaspoons salt
1 cup beef bouillon
¾ cup light rum
1½ cups sliced carrots
8 small white onions
⅛ teaspoon thyme
3 whole cloves
1 bay leaf
3 crushed peppercorns

Cut bacon slices in quarters and fry until done but not crisp. Place in bottom of 2-quart casserole. Sprinkle beef with flour and salt and brown in bacon fat, turning to brown all sides. Add with remaining ingredients to bacon in casserole. Cover and bake in a 300° F. oven for about 2 hours or until beef is tender.

Makes 4 servings.

BEEF LA JOLLA

1½ pounds beef chuck cut in 2-inch cubes
¾ cup Burgundy or Chianti wine
1½ cans (10½ ounces) condensed consommé
1 teaspoon salt
⅛ teaspoon freshly ground pepper
1 large onion, sliced
6 tablespoons fine, dry bread crumbs
6 tablespoons all purpose flour

Combine beef with wine, consommé, salt, pepper, and onion in 2-quart casserole. Mix crumbs and flour and stir into beef mixture. Cover and bake in a 300° F. oven for about 3 hours or until beef is tender.

Makes 4 servings.

BEEF BERNE

1 pound beef round steak, ¼ inch thick
½ teaspoon salt
¼ teaspoon freshly ground pepper
3 tablespoons vegetable oil
½ cup chopped onion
2 cups green pepper strips
½ teaspoon basil
3 cups soft bread crumbs
1 can (10½ ounces) condensed cream-of-mushroom
     soup
½ soup-can water
2 cups shredded Swiss cheese

Cut steak in ½-inch strips. Season with salt and pepper. Brown steak in vegetable oil in skillet. Add onions and sauté until tender. Add green pepper and basil and cook 5 minutes longer. Alternate two layers each of meat mixture and 2 cups breadcrumbs in a buttered 1½-quart casserole. Mix soup and water and pour over meat mixture in casserole and sprinkle cheese over top. Top with remaining cup of breadcrumbs. Bake in a 350° F. oven for 20 to 30 minutes.

This casserole can be prepared in advance, refrigerated, and cooked when ready to serve. Add 15 minutes to the cooking time.

Makes 6 servings.

HUNGARIAN BEEF GOULASH

2 pounds boneless beef cut in 1-inch cubes
¼ cup oil
2 cups coarsely chopped onion
1½ teaspoons salt
2 tablespoons paprika
½ cup chopped green pepper
3 tomatoes, peeled and chopped
½ cup water

Brown beef in hot oil in casserole. Add onion and continue cooking until onion is lightly browned. Add salt, paprika and green pepper and continue cooking until pepper is tender. Add tomatoes and water. Cover and cook in a 300° F. oven for 2 hours or until beef is tender.

You may serve with buttered noodles or boiled potatoes.

Makes 4 to 6 servings.

BEEF IN PORT WINE

4 slices bacon
1 large onion, sliced
2½ pounds beef chuck cut in 2-inch cubes
¼ cup flour
1½ teaspoons salt
Freshly ground pepper to taste
3 cloves garlic, finely chopped
2 cups tawny port wine
1 cup beef bouillon

Brown bacon in skillet. Remove, drain on towels and cut into small pieces. Fry onion in bacon fat until tender. Remove from skillet. Coat beef with flour that has been mixed with salt and pepper. Brown in bacon fat with garlic. Put bacon, onion and beef in buttered 2-quart casserole. Add wine and bouillon to skillet and heat and scrape brown crust from skillet. Cover and cook in a 300° F. oven for 2 to 2½ hours or until beef is tender.

You may wish to serve with boiled potatoes and buttered carrots.

Makes 4 to 6 servings.

BAKED STUFFED BEEF, ARGENTINA

1 (about 1¾ pounds) flank steak
1 teaspoon salt
¼ teaspoon freshly ground pepper
1 quart bread cubes, without crust
1 cup milk
1 teaspoon Worcestershire sauce
1½ cup cooked mixed vegetables, drained
½ cup diced green pepper
½ cup diced pimiento
2 hard-cooked eggs, chopped
1 cup beef bouillon

Have butcher trim fat from flank steak and split crosswise to open into a butterfly shape. Pound meat until thin. Season with salt and pepper. Soak bread in milk and Worcestershire sauce and spread over meat. Combine vegetables with hard-cooked eggs and spoon over bread mixture on meat. Roll up, starting at short end of meat. Tie with string or skewers. Place meat in buttered flat casserole, add bouillon and bake in a 350° F. oven for 1 hour (medium) or longer, depending on desired doneness of meat. Baste with bouillon several times. Slice crosswise to serve.

Makes 4 to 6 servings.

DEVILED BEEF

6 to 8 slices cold roast beef
Salt and freshly ground pepper to taste
¼ cup dairy sour cream
¼ cup mayonnaise
1 tablespoon grated onion
1½ tablespoons prepared mustard
Dash Tabasco
3 tablespoons dry breadcrumbs, buttered

Arrange roast beef slices in buttered flat casserole, slightly overlapping. (If beef is sliced very thin, fold slices in half.) Season to taste with salt and pepper. Mix sour cream with mayonnaise, onions and seasonings. Spread over beef slices. Sprinkle with breadcrumbs. Bake in a 400° F. oven 15 to 20 minutes or until beef is thoroughly heated and crumbs are browned.

French-fried onions make a good accompaniment.

Makes 4 to 6 servings.

SAVORY BEEF

2 medium onions, sliced
3 tablespoons shortening
2 cups leftover diced cooked beef
1 tablespoon flour
1 can (1 pound) stewed tomatoes
½ cup red Burgundy or Chianti wine
¼ cup water
1 can (2 ounces) sliced pimientos
¾ teaspoon salt
¼ teaspoon oregano
⅛ teaspoon pepper
3 cups cooked macaroni, drained
1½ cups (6 ounces) shredded natural Cheddar cheese

In a skillet, cook onions in shortening until golden. Stir in beef and brown quickly over high heat, turning frequently. Stir in flour, then add tomatoes, wine, water, pimiento, salt, oregano and pepper. Simmer a few minutes until slightly thickened. In a 1½-quart casserole layer macaroni, meat mixture and cheese. Repeat, ending with cheese. Bake in a 400° F. oven 20 minutes or until hot and bubbly. This casserole can be prepared in advance, refrigerated and baked at serving time. Add 15 minutes to baking time.

Makes 4 to 6 servings.

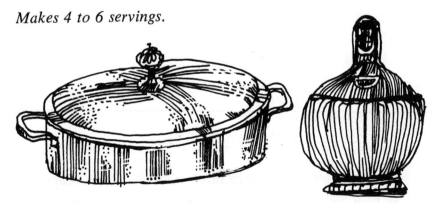

BEEF DENNIS

¾ cup rice
3 cups boiling water
1 pound ground beef chuck
2 cups chopped celery
½ cup chopped onion
2 tablespoons butter
1 tablespoon brown sugar
⅓ cup soy sauce
1 can (4 ounces) sliced mushrooms and liquid
½ cup chopped cashew nuts

Combine rice with boiling water in a 2-quart casserole. Brown beef, celery and onion in butter and mix with sugar, soy sauce, mushrooms and liquid into rice in casserole. Cover and bake in a 350° F. oven for 1 hour and 15 minutes. Remove cover. Sprinkle cashew nuts on top and bake 15 minutes longer.

Makes 4 servings.

BEEF BAKED WITH BEANS

3- or 4-pound brisket of beef
1 pound dried pea beans
½ teaspoon soda
½ teaspoon mustard
½ cup brown sugar
½ cup maple syrup
½ teaspoon salt
¼ teaspoon freshly ground pepper

Trim brisket of as much fat as possible. Wash beans and cover with water and soak overnight. Add soda and bring to a boil. Cook 10 minutes. Drain and rinse with cold water. Place beans in buttered 3-quart casserole and add mustard, sugar, maple syrup, salt and pepper. Arrange beef brisket on top and pour boiling water over beans and brisket to cover. Bake covered in a 350° F. oven until beans and brisket are tender, about 3 hours. Add additional water as necessary. Uncover last 15 minutes.

Makes 6 servings.

BEEF AND EGGPLANT

1 medium eggplant
3 tablespoons olive oil
3 medium onions, sliced
1 garlic clove, minced
3 cups finely chopped cooked beef
¾ teaspoon salt
1 teaspoon oregano
½ teaspoon thyme
1 cup chopped, peeled fresh tomatoes
½ cup dry white wine
½ cup buttered crumbs

Cut washed eggplant lengthwise into ½-inch-thick slices. Heat oil in skillet and lightly brown eggplant slices. Reserve. Add onion to skillet and cook until tender but not browned. Add garlic, beef, salt, oregano, thyme, tomatoes and wine. Cook about 30 minutes. Stir in ¼ cup crumbs. Arrange alternate layers of sauce and eggplant in a buttered 2½-quart casserole. Sprinkle buttered crumbs on top. Bake in a 350° F. oven about 1 hour. This casserole may be prepared in advance, refrigerated, and baked at serving time. Add 15 minutes to baking time.

Makes 4 servings.

STEAK AND MUSHROOMS

2 tablespoons butter
1 pound minute steaks
½ cup chopped onion
½ cup dry white wine
1 teaspoon salt
1 teaspoon Worcestershire sauce
1 can (3 ounces) chopped mushrooms and liquid

Heat butter in skillet and brown meat quickly on both sides. Transfer to buttered shallow casserole. Add onion to remaining butter in skillet and sauté until tender but not browned. Add remaining ingredients and heat and scrape brown crust from skillet. Pour over steak in casserole. Bake in a 400° F. oven for 45 minutes or until tender.

Makes 2 servings.

TIP: You might put two baking potatoes in the oven about fifteen minutes before the casserole goes in. Baked potato goes well with this dish.

STEAK BRUSSELS

¼ cup flour
½ teaspoon salt
Dash freshly ground pepper
1½ pounds minute steaks
2 tablespoons butter
1 envelope (1⅜ ounces) dehydrated onion soup
1 can (12 ounces) ale
⅛ teaspoon dill seed
2 cups diced raw potatoes
1 cup coarsley chopped celery

Mix flour with salt and pepper and coat steak with mixture. Heat butter in skillet and quickly brown meat on both sides. Transfer to a 1½-quart buttered casserole. Add onion soup and ale to skillet and bring to a boil, scraping brown crust from skillet. Add dill seed. Arrange potatoes and celery in casserole with meat. Pour hot soup mixture over casserole and cover. Bake in a 300° F. oven for 2 hours.

Makes 4 to 6 servings.

STEAK AND KIDNEY PIE

2 pounds ½-inch-thick beef rump steak
1 pound veal kidneys
¼ cup butter
2 tablespoons chopped green onions
⅛ teaspoon clove
½ teaspoon marjoram
½ teaspoon savory
1 cut-up bay leaf
1½ teaspoons salt
Freshly ground pepper to taste
¼ cup sherry
¾ cup beef bouillon
2 tablespoons butter
2 tablespoons flour
Puff pastry

Cut beef into 1½-inch cubes. Remove fat and veins from kidneys and cut into thin slices. Heat ¼ cup butter in skillet and sauté beef and kidney until browned. Add seasonings and cook 5 minutes. Add sherry and bouillon and bring to a boil. Transfer beef and kidneys to buttered, deep 2½-quart casserole. Cream 2 tablespoons butter with flour. Blend into liquid in skillet. Cook and stir until mixture thickens and pour over meat in casserole. Cover with pastry (see below).

Seal at edges and make several vent holes in center. Bake in a 350° F. oven for about 1½ hours.

Makes 6 servings.

MOCK PUFF PASTRY

1 cup flour
½ teaspoon salt
⅓ cup shortening, chilled
2 to 3 tablespoons ice water
2 tablespoons butter

Sift flour with salt into a small bowl. Cut in shortening with two knives or a pastry blender until mixture resembles cornmeal. Gradually stir in water until mixture follows fork around bowl. Chill dough. On a pastry cloth or floured board, roll chilled dough into an oblong ⅛-inch thick. Dot surface with butter. Roll up as for jelly roll. Roll out again in an oblong and fold in sides to make 3 layers. Roll out again in same manner. Repeat two more times. Chill. When ready to bake pie, roll to fit top of casserole.

BEEF STEAK, SWISS STYLE

2 pounds beef round, cut 1 to 1½ inches thick
4 tablespoons flour
1 teaspoon salt
⅛ teaspoon freshly ground pepper
4 tablespoons butter
2 small onions, sliced
2 carrots, sliced
2 stalks celery, sliced
1 can (8 ounces) tomato sauce
1 teaspoon Worcestershire sauce
½ bay leaf

Trim fat from beef and cut into serving-size portions. Mix flour, salt and pepper and coat beef. Heat butter in skillet and brown meat on both sides. Transfer to 1½-quart buttered casserole as browned. Add vegetables, tomato sauce and seasonings to casserole. Cover and bake in a 350° F. oven about 1 hour or until meat is tender. Add more liquid if needed as meat bakes. You may want to serve with mashed potatoes.

Makes 4 to 6 servings.

STEAK LUCERNE

2½ pounds beef round steak
¼ cup flour
1½ teaspoons salt
Freshly ground pepper to taste
6 slices bacon, chopped
¾ cup chopped onion
1 clove garlic, chopped
1 cup beef bouillon
2 cups canned apple sauce
2 tablespoons vinegar
½ teaspoon thyme
1 teaspoon curry powder

Trim fat from steak and cut into serving-size pieces. Mix flour with salt and pepper and coat steak with mixture. Fry bacon, onion and garlic in skillet until bacon is crisp. Remove from skillet and brown steak in pan drippings. Transfer as browned to a buttered 2-quart casserole. Mix bacon and onion with remaining ingredients and pour over steak in casserole. Cover and bake in a 350° F. oven for 1½ to 2 hours or until steak is tender.

Makes 4 to 6 servings.

STEAK PASTA CASSEROLE

2 pounds sirloin tip or round steak
¼ cup minced onion
¼ cup butter
1 can (3 ounces) sliced mushrooms
1 bay leaf
1½ teaspoons Worcestershire sauce
2 cups cooked noodles
1 teaspoon salt
Dash freshly ground pepper
1 cup light cream or top milk
1 cup croutons
¼ cup grated Parmesan cheese

Cut meat into cubes and cook meat and onion in 2 table-spoons butter until lightly browned. Add mushroom liquid, bay leaf, Worcestershire sauce, salt and pepper. Cover and simmer 30 minutes or until meat is tender. Discard bay leaf. Add noodles, cream and remaining butter and pour into a buttered 1½-quart casserole. Sprinkle top with croutons and cheese. Bake in a 325° F. oven for 45 minutes.

Makes 4 to 6 servings.

TIPS: The meat part of this casserole can be prepared in advance and refrigerated. Mix with noodles at baking time. Add approximately 15 minutes to baking time.

BRAISED BEEF TONGUE WITH VEGETABLES

First Step:
1 (4 to 5 pounds) fresh beef tongue
Water
2 teaspoons salt
2 leeks
3 medium white turnips
2 carrots

Scrub tongue and put in kettle. Cover with water and add salt. Bring to a boil and skim. Chop leeks, peel and dice turnips and carrots. Add to beef tongue and simmer 3 hours. Remove tongue from broth. Reserve broth. Skin tongue.

Second Step:
3 tablespoons butter
3 slices bacon, cut in pieces
3 carrots, peeled and diced
6 small onions, peeled
2 cups stock from tongue
½ teaspoon thyme
1 bay leaf
1 sprig parsley
½ cup dry white wine
½ pound sliced mushrooms
½ cup Madeira wine
¼ cup brandy

Heat butter in a deep casserole and brown tongue on all sides. Add bacon, carrots and onions and brown. Add stock, thyme, bay leaf and parsley. Cover and bake in a 300° F. oven for 1 hour. Add white wine and mushrooms. Cook 15 minutes longer. Add Madeira and cook 15 minutes longer. Add brandy and flame. To serve, slice tongue and surround with vegetables.

Makes 6 servings.

OXTAIL CASSEROLE

2 oxtails (about 2½ pounds), cut in 2-inch lengths
2 tablespoons butter
1 clove garlic, finely chopped
4 medium onions, sliced
3 cups beef broth
1 medium green pepper, chopped
2 cups diced, peeled, fresh tomatoes
½ cup dry red wine
2 tablespoons pearl barley
1 teaspoon salt
Freshly ground pepper to taste
2 tablespoons chopped parsley

Wash and dry oxtails and cut off as much fat as possible. Heat butter in large skillet and brown oxtails on all sides. Add garlic and onion and cook until lightly browned. Transfer to 3-quart casserole. Add beef broth and wine to skillet and heat and scrape brown crust from skillet. Pour over meat in casserole. Add remaining ingredients except parsley. Cover and bake in a 300° F. oven for 3 hours. Stir two or three times during baking. Before serving skim off as much surface fat as possible. Sprinkle with parsley. Serve with boiled potatoes, French bread and fresh pears.

Makes 4 servings.

TAMALE PIE

Crust:
1½ cups yellow cornmeal
1½ cups cold water
1½ teaspoons salt
4½ cups boiling water
Filling:
1 tablespoon oil
1 large clove garlic, chopped
1 cup chopped onion
½ cup chopped green pepper
1 pound ground beef chuck
1 can (1 pound) tomatoes
1 cup chicken broth
1½ teaspoons salt
2 teaspoons chili powder
1 teaspoon oregano
¼ teaspoon freshly ground pepper

To make crust: Mix cornmeal with cold water and salt. Stir into boiling water, cook until thickened. Then cover and continue cooking over low heat for 10 minutes. Stir frequently. Cool, stirring occasionally.

To make filling: Heat oil in large skillet and cook garlic, onion, green pepper and beef until beef is lightly browned, stirring. Add remaining ingredients and simmer covered about 15 minutes.

Spread about ⅔ of the cornmeal around sides and bottom of a buttered 1½-quart casserole. Carefully spoon in filling. Top with remaining mush. Bake in a 350° F. oven 30 to 45 minutes. This casserole can be prepared in advance, refrigerated, and baked at serving time. Add 15 to 20 minutes to baking time.

Makes 4 servings.

SHERRIED MEATBALL CASSEROLE

6 slices bacon
½ cup onion
2 cloves garlic, minced
⅓ cup fine breadcrumbs
1 egg
1½ teaspoons salt
1½ pounds ground beef chuck
1 can (3 ounces) sliced mushrooms and liquid
1 can (10¾ ounces) cream of mushroom soup
1 cup dry sherry

Cook bacon until crisp in skillet. Remove bacon and all but 2 tablespoons of the bacon fat. Reserve remainder. Add onion and garlic to the 2 tablespoons bacon fat remaining in the skillet and cook until tender but not browned. Add with crumbs, egg and salt to ground beef and mix lightly. Form into 12 meatballs. If necessary, add some of reserved bacon fat to skillet and brown meatballs. Transfer to buttered 2-quart casserole. Mix mushrooms, soup and sherry and pour over meatballs. Crumble bacon and sprinkle on top of casserole. Bake in a 375° F. oven for 45 to 50 minutes. This casserole may be prepared in advance, refrigerated and baked at serving time. Add 15 minutes to baking time.

Makes 4 to 6 servings.

STUFFED GREEN-PEPPER CASSEROLE

3 slices bacon, diced
½ pound ground beef chuck
½ cup diced onion
½ cup diced celery
½ teaspoon chili powder
½ teaspoon salt
Dash freshly ground pepper
¼ cup rice
2 cups canned tomatoes
½ cup water
4 large green peppers

Cook bacon until crisp. Remove bacon, reserve. Brown beef, onion and celery in bacon fat. Add chili powder, salt, pepper, rice and tomatoes and bring to a boil. Cut off stem end of peppers and remove seeds. Wash. Fill pepper shells with beef mixture and place in a buttered casserole. If there is too much filling, spoon around the peppers in the casserole. Add water to casserole. Cover and bake in a 350° F. oven for 30 minutes. Uncover and sprinkle with crisp bacon and bake 15 minutes longer.

Makes 4 servings.

PORK CHOPS AND BURGUNDY RICE

4 thick pork chops
1 teaspoon salt
Freshly ground pepper to taste
2 tablespoons butter
½ teaspoon poultry seasoning
4 thick slices Bermuda onion
4 rings green pepper ½-inch thick
½ cup rice
2 cans (8 ounces each) tomato sauce
¾ cup Burgundy wine

Sprinkle pork chops with salt and pepper and brown on both sides in butter. Transfer to a buttered shallow casserole. Sprinkle with poultry seasoning and place a slice of onion and a ring of green pepper on each chop. Sprinkle rice around chops. In the skillet, mix tomato sauce with wine and bring to a boil. Scrape brown crust from skillet. Pour over pork chops and rice. Cover and bake in a 350° F. oven for 1½ to 2 hours.

Makes 4 servings.

PORK CHOPS SALISBURY

6 pork chops, trimmed
1 can (10½ ounces) condensed cream-of-mushroom soup
¼ teaspoon thyme
1 can (1 pound) cut green beans, drained
1 can (7 ounces) whole kernel corn, drained
¼ teaspoon salt
1 teaspoon chili powder
⅛ teaspoon freshly ground pepper

Trim excess fat from pork chops. Brown on both sides in skillet and remove from pan. Drain off excess fat and blend in soup and thyme. Stir in beans and corn. Pour into buttered 2-quart casserole and arrange pork chops on top. Sprinkle with salt, chili powder and pepper. Cover and bake in a 350° F. oven 45 minutes or until chops are tender. Uncover and cook 15 to 20 minutes longer. This casserole can be prepared in advance, refrigerated and baked at serving time. Add 15 minutes to baking time.

Makes 6 servings.

PORK CHOPS INDIANA

4 smoked pork chops
1 can (8½ ounces) whole-kernel corn
1 cup bread cubes
½ teaspoon salt
⅛ teaspoon freshly ground pepper
½ teaspoon sage
1 tablespoon parsley flakes
1 tablespoon instant onion
1¼ cups diced peeled apple
2 tablespoons butter, melted

Brown pork chops on both sides. Drain corn, save ¼ cup liquid and lightly mix corn and ¼ cup liquid with remaining ingredients. Spoon into buttered shallow 1½-quart casserole. Arrange chops on top of mixture. Cover and bake in a 350° F. oven for 45 minutes. Uncover and bake 10 minutes longer.

Makes 4 servings.

PORK-CHOP POTATO CASSEROLE

4 thick pork chops
1 tablespoon butter
1 teaspoon salt
Dash freshly ground pepper
1 quart peeled and sliced potatoes
2 tablespoons flour
2 tablespoons grated onion
½ cup finely chopped celery
1 teaspoon salt
2 cups milk
2 tablespoons orange marmalade

Brown pork chops on both sides in butter and season with 1 teaspoon salt and pepper. Place half the potatoes in a buttered 1½-quart casserole. Sprinkle with half the flour, onion and celery and half the 1 teaspoon salt. Top with remaining potatoes, flour, salt, onion and celery. Pour milk over potatoes. Arrange pork chops on top of potatoes. Cover and bake in a 350° F. oven for 30 minutes. Uncover. Spread orange marmalade on pork chops. Continue baking another 30 minutes or until pork chops and potatoes are tender.

Makes 4 servings.

PORK TAIWAN

1 piece (about 4 pounds) center-cut pork loin, boned
Cold water
4 bay leaves
¼ cup lemon juice
3 green onions, chopped
½ teaspoon sage
½ teaspoon rosemary
1 teaspoon salt
1 egg, beaten
2 tablespoons milk
¾ cup dry breadcrumbs
Sauce:
2 cups beef bouillon
2 tablespoons bitter orange marmalade
2 tablespoons currant jelly
2 tablespoons cherry preserves
½ teaspoon grated lemon rind
¼ teaspoon cloves
½ teaspoon cinnamon
2 tablespoons lemon juice
¼ cup dry sherry

Have butcher bone and tie pork loin. Cut into 3-inch pieces. Cover with cold water and add bay leaves, lemon juice, chopped onions, sage, rosemary and salt. Cover and simmer until meat is tender, about 1½ hours. Drain and cool. Cut into ½-inch slices. Mix egg with milk and dip slices in milk mixture, then in breadcrumbs. Place on buttered shallow casserole, slightly overlapping slices. Bake in a 425° F. oven 10 to 12 minutes or until lightly browned. Mix together the boiling beef bouillon with remaining ingredients to make sauce. Serve hot.

Makes 4 servings.

EXOTIC PORK

1 cup prunes (about 20)
1½ cups water
1 cup firmly packed brown sugar
1 teaspoon grated lemon peel
1 tablespoon chopped crystallized ginger
¼ teaspoon nutmeg or mace
Dash salt
6 yams, cooked, peeled, and halved (or 2 cans [1 pound
     each] yams, drained)
1 lemon, sliced
1 orange, sliced
6 pork chops, lightly browned

Simmer prunes in water 5 to 8 minutes. Drain liquid into saucepan and mix in sugar, lemon peel, ginger, nutmeg and salt. Simmer, stirring occasionally until syrup is slightly reduced and thickened. Pit prunes. Arrange yams, prunes, lemon and orange slices in a buttered 2-quart casserole. Pour syrup over yam mixture and arrange pork chops on top. Bake in a 350° F. oven for 30 to 40 minutes or until chops are tender. Occasionally spoon syrup over yams and fruit. This casserole can be prepared in advance, refrigerated and baked at serving time. Add 15 to 20 minutes to cooking time.

Makes 4 to 6 servings.

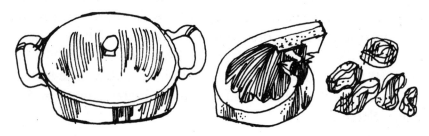

PORK AND BEER CASSEROLE

4 cups cubed, cooked pork
½ cup chopped onion
¼ cup chopped celery
1 can (12 ounces) beer
1½ cups dark rye-bread crumbs
¼ teaspoon sugar
¼ teaspoon thyme
¼ teaspoon dill weed
1 teaspoon salt

Trim fat from pork and try out in skillet. Add onion and celery and sauté until tender but not browned. Combine with cubed pork and remaining ingredients. Place in a buttered 1½-quart casserole. Cover and bake in a 375° F. oven about 40 minutes.

Makes 6 servings.

PORK À LA TAMPA

1 cup chopped celery
½ cup chopped onion
3 tablespoons cooking oil
2 cups orange juice
4 cups cubed rye bread
3 cups cubed cooked pork
¼ teaspoon thyme
¼ teaspoon ginger
1 can (8 ounces) grapefruit sections, drained

Cook celery and onion in oil until tender. Add orange juice and let simmer 5 minutes, stirring occasionally. Meanwhile, toast rye bread in a 300° F. oven until dry but not browned, about 10 minutes. Add pork and seasonings to orange-juice mixture. Alternate layers of bread cubes in a buttered 1½-quart casserole. Bake in a 350° F. oven 20 minutes. Garnish with grapefruit sections.

Makes 4 servings.

PORK, SPANISH STYLE

¼ cup flour
1 teaspoon salt
⅛ teaspoon freshly ground pepper
2 pounds boneless pork, diced
2 tablespoons olive oil
1 clove garlic, diced
3 medium potatoes, peeled and sliced
3 white turnips, peeled and sliced
1 green pepper, seeded and diced
1 red pepper, seeded and diced
1 can (1 pound) tomatoes
1 teaspoon Worcestershire sauce
1 cup beef bouillon

Mix flour with salt and pepper and coat pork. Heat olive oil in skillet and brown meat and garlic. In a buttered 3-quart casserole, place alternate layers of meat and vegetables. Mix tomatoes and Worcestershire sauce with bouillon and pour over mixture and bake in a 350° F. oven 1½ to 2 hours.

Makes 4 to 6 servings.

HAM AND APPLES EN CASSEROLE

2 slices ham, ½ inch thick
3 tart apples
½ cup raisins
½ cup brown sugar
1 cup apple juice

Trim fat from ham and arrange one slice in a buttered flat casserole. Peel apples, core, and chop finely. Mix with raisins and brown sugar. Spoon on ham in casserole. Top with second ham slice. Pour apple juice around ham. Bake in a 400° F. oven about 30 minutes, basting several times.

Makes 4 to 6 servings.

HAM SCALLOP

1 can (4 ounces) sliced mushrooms, drained
2 tablespoons chopped onion
2 tablespoons chopped green pepper
1 small clove garlic, minced
Dash thyme
2 tablespoons butter or margarine
1 can (10½ ounces) condensed cream-of-chicken soup
2 cups cooked spaghetti
1½ cups diced cooked ham
1 cup canned tomatoes

Cook mushrooms, onion, green pepper, garlic, and thyme in butter until tender. Combine with remaining ingredients. Pour into buttered 1½-quart casserole. Bake in a 350° F. oven 30 minutes or until cooked through. This casserole can be prepared in advance, refrigerated and baked at serving time. Add 15 minutes to baking time.

Makes 2 servings.

HAM–LIMA BEAN SUPPER CASSEROLE

½ cup chopped onion
3 tablespoons butter or margarine
1 teaspoon MSG
1 tablespoon flour
1 teaspoon salt
⅛ teaspoon freshly ground pepper
1 can (1 pound) tomatoes
1 can (1 pound) lima beans, drained
2 cups diced cooked ham
1½ cups buttered, soft breadcrumbs

Cook onion in butter until tender. Add MSG, flour, salt, pepper and tomatoes. Blend thoroughly and cook and stir until mixture boils and is thickened. Add lima beans and diced ham and heat. Pour into a buttered 1½-quart casserole. Sprinkle breadcrumbs around outside edge of top. Bake in a 425° F. oven 15 minutes or until crumbs are lightly browned. This casserole can be prepared in advance, refrigerated and baked at serving time. Add 20 minutes to baking time.

Makes 4 to 6 servings.

BAKED SPARERIBS WITH RICE

2½ pounds spareribs
1 teaspoon salt
Freshly ground pepper to taste
1 tablespoon cornstarch
1 tablespoon brown sugar
1 cup Burgundy wine
1 cup crushed pineapple and juice
1 tablespoon soy sauce
3 cups hot cooked rice

Have spareribs cut into serving-size sections. Arrange meaty side up in a large shallow baking pan. Sprinkle with salt and pepper. Bake in a 350° F. oven for 1 hour. Meanwhile mix cornstarch with sugar in a small saucepan. Add wine, pineapple and soy sauce and bring to a boil, stirring. Spoon rice into a shallow buttered casserole. Arrange spareribs on top. Spoon half of sauce over spareribs and rice. Continue baking 15 minutes. Spoon over remaining sauce and bake 15 minutes longer.

Makes 4 servings.

SAUSAGE AU VIN BLANC

1 pound link sausage
1½ cups dry white wine
1 grated carrot
1 stalk celery, finely chopped
½ cup consommé

Cook sausage until partially done to remove some of the fat. Combine remaining ingredients and simmer 10 minutes in a casserole. Add sausage and bake in a 300° F. oven for about 45 minutes.

Makes 2 to 3 servings.

SAUSAGE SAUERKRAUT CASSEROLE

2 pounds pork-sausage meat
2 cups sauerkraut, drained
2 tablespoons brown sugar
1 teaspoon celery seed
2½ cups (5-ounce package) medium noodles
2 cups beef bouillon
½ cup buttered breadcrumbs

Form sausages into 12 patties and brown on both sides. Reserve 2 tablespoons sausage fat. Cook noodles in boiling salted water, as directed on package. Drain and mix with reserved sausage fat. Spoon half the noodles into a buttered 1½-quart casserole. Mix sauerkraut with brown sugar and celery seed and place half on noodles and top with half the sausage patties. Repeat, ending with sausage. Pour bouillon over casserole and top with breadcrumbs. Bake in a 350° F. oven 45 to 50 minutes.

Makes 4 to 6 servings.

FRUITED SAUSAGE PUFFS

1 pound link sausage
2 cans (1 pound each) yams, drained
¼ cup melted butter
2 cups canned apple sauce
3 egg yolks
1 can (13½ ounces) pineapple tidbits, drained
1 teaspoon grated lemon rind
½ teaspoon nutmeg
⅓ cup maple syrup
3 egg whites, stiffly beaten
⅓ cup sliced blanched almonds

Cook sausages until lightly browned. Drain and reserve. Mash yams and beat in butter, apple sauce, and egg yolks, mixing until well blended. Fold in pineapple, lemon rind, nutmeg and maple syrup. Fold in egg whites and pile mixture lightly into a buttered 1½-quart casserole. Place sausages on top of casserole to form spokes. Bake in a 350° F. oven 25 to 30 minutes or until potatoes are lightly browned. Sprinkle with almonds 5 minutes before removing from oven.

Makes 6 servings.

CHIVE SAUSAGE EL DORADO

1½ pounds link sausage
1 cup green pepper, chopped
1 can (1 pound) canneloni beans, drained
3 cups cooked rice
¼ cup chopped chives
1 can (6 ounces) tomato paste
1 can (1 pound) tomatoes, chopped
Salt and freshly ground pepper

Cook sausage until lightly browned. Reserve ¼ cup of the pan drippings. Fry green pepper in the ¼-cup drippings until tender. Combine with remaining ingredients, season to taste with salt and pepper and pour into a buttered 1½-quart casserole. Arrange sausages on top. Bake in a 400° F. oven 25 to 30 minutes or until bubbly.

Makes 6 servings.

LANCASTER SAUERKRAUT

1 can (12 ounces) luncheon meat
¼ cup butter
¾ cup chopped onion
2 cloves garlic, diced
2 tablespoons flour
2 teaspoons sugar
1 can (10½ ounces) condensed beef broth
1 cup tomato juice
3 tablespoons tomato paste
1 can (1 pound 11 ounces) sauerkraut, drained
1 cup dairy sour cream

Cut luncheon meat into ¼-inch-thick slices and then into strips. Heat butter in large skillet and brown meat and onion and garlic. Stir in flour and sugar. Add broth, tomato juice and paste and cook and stir until mixture comes to a boil and is thickened. Arrange sauerkraut in bottom of buttered 2½-quart casserole. Cover with meat and sauce. Bake in a 350° F. oven about 40 minutes. Spoon sour cream over top, swirling lightly into mixture.

Makes 4 servings.

SYRIAN LAMB CASSEROLE

2½ pounds boneless lamb, cut in thin slices
2 large onions, sliced
3 tablespoons oil
1 teaspoon salt
Freshly ground pepper to taste
¼ teaspoon nutmeg
⅛ teaspoon cinnamon
2 large eggplants
2½ cups (approximately) tomato juice

Trim fat from lamb and cut into small pieces. Brown with onion in 1 tablespoon of oil. Add seasonings. Peel eggplant and cut into 1-inch slices. Fry in remaining oil until almost tender. Arrange layers of eggplant slices and meat mixture in a buttered 2-quart casserole. Pour tomato juice over eggplant and lamb to cover. Bake in a 325° F. oven until almost dry, about 1 hour. Serve over hot cooked rice.

Makes 6 servings.

LAMB CURRY

2½ pounds boneless lamb, cut in 1-inch cubes
¼ cup butter
1 clove garlic, chopped
1 cup chopped onion
1 cup chopped, peeled apple
3 tablespoons curry powder
½-inch piece ginger root, grated (or ½ teaspoon ground ginger)
½ cup flour
3 cups chicken broth
1 good-size tomato, peeled and chopped
1 can (4 ounces) flaked coconut
1½ cups milk
Salt and freshly ground pepper to taste

Brown lamb in butter in skillet. Transfer to 2½- to 3-quart casserole. Add garlic, onion, apple, curry and ginger and cook slowly until onions and apples are tender but not browned. Stir in flour and gradually stir in chicken broth. Cook and stir until mixture boils and is thickened. Add tomato. Pour over lamb in casserole. Cover and bake in a 325° F. oven for 1 hour or until lamb is tender. Meanwhile, simmer coconut in milk for 20 minutes. Strain, pressing all milk from coconut. When lamb is tender, stir milk into curry mixture, add salt and pepper to taste, and let cook another 10 minutes. Serve over cooked rice.

Makes 4 to 6 servings.

TIP: Accompany with chopped cashew nuts, toasted shredded coconut, chutney, chopped onion and raisins.

ZUCCHINI AND LAMB, TEHERAN

6 medium-size zucchini
Salt and freshly ground pepper
2 tablespoons olive oil
¾ cup chopped onion
1 clove garlic, finely chopped
1½ pounds ground lamb
¼ cup rice
1 teaspoon salt
Freshly ground pepper to taste
1 teaspoon grated lemon rind
2 tablespoons chopped fresh mint (or 1 teaspoon dried
   mint)
1 cup chicken broth
1 cup buttered crumbs

Scrub zucchini and cut in thin slices crosswise. Put half the slices in a buttered casserole and season with salt and pepper. Heat olive oil and sauté onion, garlic, lamb and rice until lamb is just gray, not browned. Mix in 1 teaspoon salt, pepper, lemon rind and mint. Spoon over zucchini and top with remaining zucchini. Pour broth over zucchini and lamb in casserole. Sprinkle with crumbs. Bake in a 375° F. oven 25 to 30 minutes.

Makes 4 to 6 servings.

BRAISED LAMB WITH SOUR CREAM

2 pounds lamb shoulder, diced
2 tablespoons olive oil
1 clove garlic, minced
½ cup chopped onion
1 tablespoon paprika
1 teaspoon salt
1 can (16 ounces) tomato sauce
1 teaspoon Worcestershire sauce
⅛ teaspoon rosemary
1 cup dairy sour cream

Trim fat from lamb. Heat olive oil in skillet and brown lamb, garlic and onion. Transfer to a buttered 2-quart casserole and sprinkle with paprika and salt. Add tomato sauce, Worcestershire and rosemary to skillet and heat. Scrape to remove brown crust from skillet. Pour tomato mixture over lamb in casserole. Cover and bake in a 300° F. oven for 2 hours or until tender. When ready to serve, stir in sour cream.

Makes 4 to 6 servings.

LAMB BROCCOLI CASSEROLE

2 tablespoons butter
2 tablespoons flour
1 cup milk
1 cup shredded natural Cheddar cheese
½ teaspoon salt
¼ teaspoon celery seed
¼ teaspoon dry mustard
⅛ teaspoon pepper
½ teaspoon Worcestershire sauce
Sliced cooked lamb for 4 servings (about 1 pound)
1 package (10 ounces) frozen broccoli, cooked, drained
1 medium tomato, peeled and thinly sliced
¼ cup shredded process American cheese

Cook butter and flour together until bubbly. Slowly stir in milk and cook and stir until mixture boils and is thickened. Remove from heat. Add Cheddar cheese and seasonings. Stir until cheese is melted. Arrange layers of lamb, broccoli and tomato slices in 1½-quart shallow casserole. Pour sauce over all. Bake in a 350° F. oven 15 minutes. Sprinkle with American cheese and bake 5 minutes longer.

Makes 4 servings.

DENVER LAMB CASSEROLE

¼ cup butter
1 clove garlic
1½ pounds lamb-stew meat, cubed
3 cups cubed potatoes
4 medium onions, sliced
1 bay leaf, crushed
1 teaspoon salt
⅛ teaspoon freshly ground pepper
½ teaspoon marjoram
1 cup bouillon
½ cup seasoned breadcrumbs

Heat butter and garlic in skillet and brown lamb on all sides. Mix with remaining ingredients except crumbs. Spoon into a buttered 2½-quart casserole. Cover and bake in a 350° F. oven for 2 hours or until tender. Remove cover and sprinkle top with crumbs in the last 15 minutes.

Makes 4 servings.

CASSOULET

1 quart pea beans
2 quarts water
3 teaspoons salt
2 cloves garlic, chopped
2 carrots, peeled and quartered
2 medium onions, peeled
Bouquet garni*
½ cup diced salt pork
3 tablespoons olive oil
1 pound lean pork, cubed
1½ pounds lean lamb, cubed
1 Bermuda onion, chopped†
¾ cup shallots, chopped†
1 cup sliced celery
1 can (8 ounces) tomato sauce
1 cup dry white wine
½ pound hard garlic sausage, sliced
1 roasted duck, meat removed from bone

Wash beans and soak overnight in water and salt. Add garlic, carrots, onions, bouquet garni, and salt pork. Bring to a boil and simmer, covered, 1 hour. Skim. While beans are cooking, heat oil in skillet and brown pork and lamb cubes. At end of hour add to beans. Cook Bermuda onion, shallots and celery until tender in pork and lamb drippings. Add tomato sauce and wine to skillet. Heat and scrape brown crust from skillet and add to beans. Add garlic sausage. Continue to simmer until meat is tender, about 1 hour. Add more water, if necessary, to cover beans. Skim off excess fat and discard bouquet garni. Add salt and pepper, if necessary. Spoon mix-

* Bouquet garni: sprig parsley, celery leaves, bay leaf, pinch thyme, and 2 cloves, all tied in cheesecloth.
† 2 cups chopped Bermuda onion may be substituted.

ture into a large 4- to 5-quart casserole and arrange pieces of duck in bean mixture. Bake in a 350° F. oven 30 to 40 minutes.

Makes 8 servings.

VEAL PARMESAN

1½ pounds thin veal cutlets
¼ cup flour
1 teaspoon salt
⅛ teaspoon freshly ground pepper
1 egg, beaten
2 tablespoons milk
1 cup dry breadcrumbs
⅓ cup olive oil
4 tablespoons butter
½ cup chopped onion
1 clove garlic, chopped
1 can (6 ounces) tomato paste
1¼ cups water
½ teaspoon basil
½ teaspoon oregano
½ teaspoon salt
4 tablespoons grated Parmesan cheese
1 package (8 ounces) mozzarella cheese, sliced

Cut veal into serving-size pieces. Mix flour with 1 teaspoon salt and pepper. Coat veal with flour mixture. Mix egg with milk and dip veal in egg, then in breadcrumbs. Brown on both sides in hot olive oil. When browned, transfer to a buttered shallow casserole. Add butter to skillet, brown onion and garlic. Add tomato paste, water, basil, oregano and ½ teaspoon salt. Bring to a boil and simmer 5 minutes. Sprinkle veal cutlets with Parmesan cheese and spoon tomato sauce over cutlets. Arrange slices of mozzarella cheese on top of cutlets and sauce. Bake in a 350° F. oven 15 to 20 minutes or until cheese is melted.

Makes 4 servings.

TIP: Spaghetti with garlic butter complements this dish.

VEAL ROLLS RISOTTO

1 package (8 ounces) sliced natural Swiss cheese
4 slices boiled ham
8 slices (about 12 ounces) veal for scallopini (pounded thin)
2 tablespoons flour
1 teaspoon salt
Freshly ground pepper to taste
3 tablespoons butter
¼ cup diced onion
2 cups hot water
1 tablespoon lemon juice
1 can (4 ounces) sliced mushrooms and liquid
1¾ cups precooked rice

Cut 2 slices cheese into 4 strips each. Cut boiled ham slices in half. On each slice of veal, arrange a piece of ham and on top of ham a strip of cheese. Fold over edges of veal and secure with toothpicks. Mix flour with salt and pepper and coat veal rolls with flour mixture. Reserve remaining flour mixture. Heat butter in skillet and lightly brown veal rolls. Remove from skillet. Fry onion until tender but not browned.

Stir in remaining flour mixture. Gradually stir in hot water, blending until smooth. Add lemon juice and mushrooms and liquid and bring to a boil. Meanwhile, cut remaining cheese into narrow strips. Combine with rice in a buttered shallow 2½-quart casserole. Pour hot mushroom mixture over rice. Arrange veal rolls on top. Cover and bake in a 400° F. oven for 20 to 25 minutes.

Makes 4 servings.

VEAL AND HAM CASSEROLE

1½ pounds boneless veal shoulder
½ pound smoked ham
4 tablespoons butter
12 small white onions
2 cups canned tomatoes
2 cups beef or chicken broth
1 cup sliced celery
1½ teaspoons salt
Freshly ground pepper to taste
½ teaspoon rosemary
3 tablespoons flour
3 tablespoons water
6 small cooked potatoes
1 cup cooked peas, drained

Cut veal into serving-size pieces and ham into strips. Brown veal in butter and transfer to buttered 2-quart casserole. Brown onions and transfer to casserole. Combine tomatoes, broth, celery and seasonings in skillet. Heat and scrape brown crust from skillet. Pour mixture over veal in casserole. Cover and bake in a 350° F. oven for 1 hour or until tender. Mix flour with water to form a thin paste. Stir into stew. Add potatoes and peas and cook 20 minutes longer.

Makes 6 servings.

VEAL À LA SEVILLE

1½ pounds veal cutlet
⅓ cup olive oil
1 teaspoon salt
Freshly ground pepper to taste
¼ cup chopped hazelnuts
4 thin slices ham
1 red onion, diced
1½ cups chopped mushrooms
¼ cup chicken broth
½ cup dry white wine
¼ cup tomato paste
½ teaspoon cloves
½ teaspoon mace
½ teaspoon thyme
¼ teaspoon saffron

Cut veal into serving-size pieces and pound thin with mallet. Heat olive oil in skillet and brown veal lightly on both sides. Transfer to buttered shallow casserole as browned. Season with salt and pepper. Layer with slices of ham. Brown hazelnuts in remaining oil and sprinkle over ham and veal. Brown onion and add remaining ingredients to skillet. Blend and pour over veal. Bake in a 400° F. oven for 15 to 20 minutes.

Makes 4 servings.

VEAL BIRDS THAMES

2 slices (about 2 pounds) veal rounds
1 teaspoon salt
Dash freshly ground pepper
6 slices bacon
½ pound ground fresh pork
½ teaspoon sage
¼ cup finely chopped onion
1½ cups soft breadcrumbs
1 cup whole milk

Cut veal steak into 6 serving-size pieces and pound thin. Season with salt and pepper. Cut bacon into ½-inch pieces and brown with pork meat. Combine with sage, onion and breadcrumbs. Put a spoonful of filling in center of each serving of veal. Roll filled veal and fasten with toothpicks. Brown in bacon fat in skillet and transfer to buttered shallow casserole. Pour milk around veal birds and bake in a 300° F. oven about 1 hour or until tender.

Makes 6 servings.

SAVORY VEAL

2 tablespoons flour
1 teaspoon salt
Dash freshly ground pepper
2 pounds veal, cubed
2 tablespoons butter
½ cup chopped onion
2 cups beef broth
1 cup chopped celery
1 cup peas, drained
½ teaspoon rosemary

Mix flour, salt and pepper and rub into veal cubes. Heat the butter in skillet and brown veal and onion. Transfer to 2-quart casserole. Heat broth in skillet and, after scraping brown crust from skillet, add to casserole. Add celery, peas and rosemary to veal in casserole. Cover and bake in a 350° F. oven for 1½ to 2 hours. Thicken gravy with additional flour if desired.

Makes 6 servings.

VEAL WITH WINE AND MUSHROOMS

2½ pounds veal for scallopini
¼ cup flour
1 teaspoon salt
⅛ teaspoon freshly ground pepper
4 tablespoons olive oil
2 cloves garlic, chopped
½ cup finely chopped onion
2 cups sliced fresh mushrooms
2 cups bouillon
2 cups dry white wine
1 teaspoon dried rosemary
3 tablespoons chopped parsley

Pound veal very thin. Mix flour with salt and pepper. Coat veal slices with flour mixture. Brown slowly on both sides in oil. As meat browns, transfer to a buttered shallow casserole. When veal is browned, add garlic, onions and mushrooms to skillet and brown lightly. Spoon over veal in casserole. Add bouillon, wine and rosemary to skillet. Heat and scrape brown crust from skillet. Pour over veal. Cover and bake in a 350° F. oven for 45 minutes. Uncover, sprinkle with parsley and bake 15 minutes longer.

Makes 6 servings.

CHICKEN WITH BACON

4 slices bacon
5 whole chicken breasts, boned
½ cup flour
1 teaspoon salt
¼ teaspoon freshly ground pepper
4 medium potatoes, peeled and cut in 1-inch cubes
1 clove garlic, crushed
½ teaspoon salt
⅛ teaspoon thyme
⅔ cup chicken broth
½ cup chopped parsley
½ cup dry white wine

Cut bacon in ½-inch pieces and cook until crisp in a large skillet. Remove from skillet. Wash and dry chicken breasts and cut into 2-inch pieces. Coat with flour that has been mixed with salt and pepper. Brown chicken in bacon fat. As pieces brown, transfer to a 2-quart casserole. Add potatoes and garlic to skillet and fry until lightly browned. Arrange with chicken pieces in casserole. Put salt, thyme and broth in skillet. Heat and scrape brown crust from skillet. Pour over chicken and scatter bacon pieces on top. Cover and bake in a 350° F. oven for 45 minutes. Add parsley and wine and bake 15 minutes longer.

Makes 4 to 6 servings.

CHICKEN HONDURAS

2 (2½ to 3 pounds) broiler-fryers, disjointed
6 bananas, peeled
2 canned or bottled hot chili peppers
2 tablespoons salad oil
1 clove garlic
1 bay leaf
¼ cup butter
1 cup chicken broth
Water
2 tablespoons flour
¼ cup cream
½ cup raisins
Salt to taste

Wash and wipe chicken pieces dry and put chicken and bananas on a pan or piece of foil. Mash chili peppers with oil, garlic and bay leaf to make a purée (or whirl in blender), adding enough oil to make the mixture a spreading consistency if necessary. Spread on chicken and bananas. Heat butter in skillet and brown chicken pieces on all sides. Transfer chicken to buttered large shallow casserole. Add remaining puréed mixture and chicken broth to butter in skillet. Heat and pour over chicken. Bake in a 400° F. oven for 20 minutes. Add bananas, basting with pan liquids, and bake for an additional 15 minutes. Arrange chicken and bananas on platter and keep hot. Measure pan gravy from casserole and add water to make 2 cups. Mix 2 tablespoons flour with ¼ cup cream and stir into liquid. Cook and stir until gravy boils and is thickened. Add raisins and salt to taste.

Makes 4 to 6 servings.

PHILIPPINE CHICKEN AND PORK

2 2½- to 3-pound broiler-fryer chickens
1 pound boneless pork
½ cup vinegar
½ cup soy sauce
½ cup finely chopped onion
2 cloves garlic, crushed
2 teaspoons paprika
6 peppercorns
1 bay leaf
½ cup butter

Cut chickens into serving-size pieces. Save backs, necks and wings for broth. Trim off fat and dice pork into small pieces. In a bowl, mix vinegar with remaining ingredients except butter. Add chicken and pork and stir to coat all pieces. Cover and let stand in refrigerator for at least 1 hour, longer if possible. Put mixture into a casserole and simmer, covered, over low heat about 30 minutes or until chicken is tender. Remove cover, add butter and continue cooking uncovered until sauce is reduced and thickened.

Makes 4 to 6 servings.

REGAL CURRIED CHICKEN

Day before serving:
1 3½-pound chicken
1 onion
1 rib celery
6 peppercorns
1 teaspoon salt

Wash and disjoint chicken. Remove meat from bones and cut into bite-size pieces. Refrigerate. Put chicken bones in saucepan. Add onion, celery, peppercorns, and salt. Cover with water. Simmer, covered, for 2 hours. Strain and reduce broth to 1½ cups. Refrigerate.

Serving day:
4 tablespoons flour
4 tablespoons butter
1 cup finely chopped onion
½ clove garlic, crushed
1½ tablespoons curry powder
½ teaspoon powdered ginger (or grated ginger root)
½ teaspoon salt
2 tablespoons chutney, chopped
¼ cup raisins
1 large cucumber, peeled and diced
¼ cup blanched almonds
1 teaspoon butter
½ cup cream
2 tablespoons lemon juice

Roll boned bits of chicken in flour and brown in 4 table-spoons butter in large skillet. Transfer from pan to a 1½-quart casserole. Brown onion and garlic, adding additional butter if necessary. Mix in curry powder, ginger, and salt. Blend in the 1½ cups chicken broth and scrape brown crust from skillet. Add chutney, raisins, and cucumbers. Pour over chicken in casserole. Cover and bake in a 350° F. oven for 1 hour or until chicken is tender. Sauté almonds in 1 tea-spoon butter until lightly browned. Put through Mouli grater or chop very finely and heat with cream. Add to curry mixture in casserole with lemon juice. Correct seasonings if necessary.

Makes 4 servings.

TIPS: This should be served with hot rice. You may also use additional chutney, coconut, raisins and chopped peanuts when serving the chicken.

CHICKEN ASPARAGUS TUCSON

4 chicken breasts
1 quart water
½ teaspoon salt
1 small onion
1 stalk celery
4 tablespoons butter
6 tablespoons flour
3 cups broth from chicken
1 cup shredded sharp Cheddar cheese
1½ pounds fresh asparagus
½ cup buttered breadcrumbs

Combine chicken breasts with water, salt, onion and celery and simmer until tender, about 30 minutes. Remove from broth and cool. Concentrate broth to 3 cups. Heat butter in saucepan, stir in flour and let bubble. Gradually stir in chicken broth and cook and stir until mixture boils and is thickened. Taste and add more salt, if necessary. Add cheese and stir until melted. Meanwhile, trim and wash asparagus and cook in boiling salted water until just barely tender. Arrange asparagus in bottom of buttered shallow casserole. Remove chicken from bone in large pieces and place on asparagus. Cover chicken and asparagus with cheese gravy. Sprinkle casserole with crumbs. Bake in a 425° F. oven for 15 to 20 minutes.

Makes 4 to 6 servings.

BUFFET CHICKEN WITH HAM ROLLS

Day before serving:
1 stewing chicken (4 to 5 pounds), cut up
1 teaspoon salt
1 large onion stuck with 3 cloves
2 stalks celery and leaves
Giblets from chicken

Put the cut-up chicken in a pot with the salt, onion, and celery. Add just enough water to cover, and simmer until tender, about 1½ hours. Cool chicken in broth and refrigerate overnight. Cook giblets separately in a small amount of water. Drain and chop. Refrigerate.

Serving day:
4 tablespoons butter
4 tablespoons flour
Salt and freshly ground pepper to taste
1 cup light cream
¼ teaspoon rosemary

Drain off the chicken broth (there should be 2 cups). Remove chicken meat in big pieces from bones, discarding skin. Place chicken in a buttered, flat large casserole. Melt butter in sauce pan. Stir in flour and cook until bubbly. Gradually add the 2 cups chicken broth and cook and stir until mixture boils and is thickened. Stir in salt and pepper, cream, rosemary, and the chopped giblets. Cook over low heat 10 minutes, stirring occasionally. Pour over chicken in casserole.

Ham Rolls:
2 cups soft breadcrumbs
¼ minced onion
2 tablespoons chopped parsley
1 teaspoon poultry seasoning
¼ teaspoon salt
6 thin slices cooked ham

Combine breadcrumbs with onion, parsley, poultry seasoning and salt. Add enough of the remaining chicken broth to moisten dressing slightly. Reserve 2 tablespoons and spoon remainder equally on ham slices. Roll ham around stuffing. Cut ham rolls in two crosswise and arrange on top of chicken and gravy. Sprinkle with reserved stuffing. Bake in a 350° F. oven for 30 minutes. This casserole can be prepared in advance, refrigerated, and cooked at serving time. Add 15 minutes to cooking time.

Makes 8 servings.

BALTIMORE CHICKEN CASSEROLE

Day before serving:
2 (2½ to 3 pounds each) broiler-fryer chickens
3 cups cold water
1 medium onion, sliced
3 celery tops
1 bay leaf
2 teaspoons salt
8 peppercorns
¼ teaspoon thyme

If desired, chickens may be cut up. Wash. Simmer chicken, covered, in water and seasonings until tender, about 45 minutes. Refrigerate chicken in broth overnight.

Serving day:
¼ cup butter
½ cup flour
1 cup light cream
1 cup sliced mushrooms
2 cups herbed bread stuffing
¼ cup butter, melted
½ cup grated sharp cheese

Remove chicken meat from bones, and dice. Should make about 5 cups diced chicken and 3 to 3½ cups broth. Heat ¼ cup butter in saucepan. Add flour and let bubble. Stir in the 3 cups chicken broth and the cream. Cook and stir until mixture comes to a boil and is thickened. Stir in mushrooms and the 5 cups diced chicken. Pour into buttered 2-quart casserole. Combine herbed bread stuffing with melted butter and sprinkle on top of chicken in casserole. Bake in a 375° F. oven 30 minutes. Sprinkle cheese on top of crumbs and bake 10 minutes longer.

Makes 8 servings.

CHICKEN AND OYSTER SUPREME

3 cups cooked chicken, coarsely diced
½ pint raw oysters, drained
2 hard-cooked eggs, sliced
½ cup minced celery
4 tablespoons butter
3 tablespoons flour
2 cups chicken broth
¼ teaspoon sage
Salt and freshly ground pepper to taste

Layer chicken, oysters and eggs in buttered 1½-quart casserole. Cook celery in butter until tender. Blend in flour and cook until bubbly. Stir in chicken broth and cook and stir until mixture boils and is thickened. Add sage and season to taste with salt and pepper. Pour over chicken in casserole. Cover and bake in a 425° F. oven for 25 minutes. This casserole can be prepared in advance, refrigerated and baked at serving time. Add 15 minutes to baking time.

Makes 6 servings.

ORANGE CHICKEN

1 (2½ to 3 pounds) broiler-fryer cut up
¼ cup flour
1 teaspoon salt
⅛ teaspoon freshly ground pepper
½ cup shortening (half butter)
½ cup sliced onions
½ can (6 ounces) frozen orange-juice concentrate
½ cup water
2 tablespoons flour
½ teaspoon sugar

Wash and dry chicken and coat with ¼ cup flour that has been mixed with salt and pepper. Heat shortening in skillet and brown chicken pieces over moderately high heat. Remove to 1½-quart casserole. When all chicken is browned, fry onion rings in remaining fat until tender but not browned. Arrange over chicken. Mix orange juice with water and pour over chicken. Cover and bake in a 350° F. oven for about 1 hour or until tender. Remove chicken and make gravy with flour and sugar, adding additional water if necessary. Serve chicken at once with gravy.

Makes 4 servings.

CHICKEN NATALIE

2 pounds chicken breasts and thighs
2 tablespoons shortening
1 can (10½ ounces) condensed cream-of-chicken soup
½ soup-can milk
¼ teaspoon poultry seasoning
¼ teaspoon salt
Dash freshly ground pepper
4 medium carrots, cut lengthwise in quarters
6 small onions
1 package (10 ounces) frozen lima beans

Brown chicken in shortening and place in 2-quart casserole. Stir soup, milk and seasonings together and heat. Add carrots and onions to soup mixture, cover and cook over low heat 10 minutes, stirring often. Add lima beans and cook until separated, stirring often. Pour over chicken in casserole. Cover. Immediately refrigerate until 1 hour and 15 minutes before serving time. Bake, covered, in a 375° F. oven for 1 hour. Uncover and bake 15 minutes longer or until chicken is tender. If not refrigerated before cooking, decrease baking time of covered casserole 15 minutes.

Makes 4 servings.

CHICKEN BREASTS MEDITERRANEAN

3 whole broiler-fryer chicken breasts, cut in half
1½ teaspoons MSG
½ teaspoon salt
¼ teaspoon paprika
½ cup butter
½ cup chopped onion
1 clove garlic, chopped
1 green pepper, cut in strips
1 medium eggplant, cut in ½-inch slices
2 zucchini, cut in ½-inch slices
3 large tomatoes, peeled and cut in pieces
¼ teaspoon Tabasco
¼ teaspoon thyme
¼ teaspoon oregano
2 tablespoons chopped parsley

Sprinkle chicken with 1 teaspoon MSG, salt and paprika. Heat butter in skillet. Brown chicken breasts on both sides and remove. Add onion, garlic, and green pepper and cook until tender but not browned. Remove. Brown eggplant slices on both sides, a few at a time, in skillet. Add zucchini and tomatoes to skillet and cook rapidly until tomatoes are cooked down and part of the liquid is evaporated. Add cooked onion, garlic and green pepper with remaining ½ teaspoon MSG and herbs. Mix well and spoon half of the mixture into a 4-quart casserole. Arrange chicken breasts over vegetables. Spoon remaining vegetables around chicken breasts. Bake uncovered in a 375° F. oven for 45 minutes or until chicken is tender. Baste several times with liquid from vegetables.

Makes 6 servings.

ARROZ CON POLLO (Chicken with Rice)

1 broiler-fryer chicken, cut in serving-size pieces
1 teaspoon MSG
1½ teaspoons salt
½ teaspoon paprika
¼ cup salad oil
½ cup chopped onion
1 can (1 pound) tomatoes
1 can (1 pound) peas
2 bouillon cubes
¼ teaspoon saffron
1½ cups cooked rice

Sprinkle chicken with MSG, 1 teaspoon of the salt, and the paprika. Brown in hot oil in skillet. Remove chicken to a baking dish that can be covered tightly. Add onion to skillet and cook until tender but not browned. Drain liquid from tomatoes and peas and add enough water to make 3 cups. Stir into skillet and scrape brown pieces from bottom with a spoon. Add bouillon cubes, saffron and remaining ½ teaspoon salt and bring to a boil. Pour over chicken. Sprinkle rice around chicken, stirring so all of rice is moistened. Add tomatoes and cover tightly. Bake in a 350° F. oven for 25 minutes. Uncover and toss rice. Add peas. Cover and bake 10 minutes longer.

Makes 4 servings.

CHICKEN AND NOODLES

¼ cup butter
¼ cup flour
1 teaspoon salt
2 cups chicken stock
2 cups milk
1 can (6 or 8 ounces) sliced mushrooms
¼ cup sherry
½ teaspoon marjoram
2 tablespoons chopped chives
1 package (8 ounces) medium noodles, cooked according to package directions
5 cups diced cooked chicken
¼ cup grated Parmesan cheese

Melt butter in saucepan. Add flour and salt and let cook until bubbly. Gradually stir in chicken stock, milk and liquid from mushrooms. Cook and stir until mixture boils and is thickened. Add sherry, marjoram and chives. Mix with noodles and chicken. Spoon into a buttered 3-quart casserole. Sprinkle with grated cheese. Bake in a 350° F. oven for 25 to 30 minutes. This casserole can be prepared in advance, refrigerated and cooked at serving time. Increase cooking time 15 to 20 minutes.

Makes 8 servings.

HELEN'S QUICK CHICKEN DIVAN

2 cups dairy sour cream
1 envelope (1⅜ ounces) onion-soup mix
2 packages (10 ounces each) frozen broccoli spears, cooked, drained
2 cups coarsely cut cooked chicken
1 cup cream, whipped
2 tablespoons grated Parmesan cheese

Mix sour cream with onion soup. Arrange broccoli in a buttered shallow casserole. Spoon half the sauce over the broccoli. Cover with chicken. Fold whipped cream into remainder of sour cream mixture and spoon over chicken. Bake in a 375° F. oven for 20 to 25 minutes or until hot and bubbly. Sprinkle with Parmesan cheese.

Makes 4 servings.

MANDARIN CHICKEN

1 can (10½ ounces) condensed cream-of-mushroom soup
½ soup-can milk
2 cups (8 ounces) shredded sharp natural Cheddar cheese
1 teaspoon soy sauce
2 cups cooked rice
2 cups diced cooked chicken
1 can (8 ounces) water chestnuts, drained, sliced
1 can (3 ounces) sliced mushrooms, drained
1 can (3 ounces) chow-mein noodles

Mix soup and milk and heat. Add cheese and soy sauce and stir until cheese is melted. Combine rice with chicken, water chestnuts and mushrooms. Alternate layers of sauce and rice mixture in a 2-quart casserole. Arrange noodles around top edge of mixture. Bake in a 350° F. oven 25 minutes.

Makes 4 servings.

RIVIERA CHICKEN CASSEROLE

1 package (8 ounces) long spaghetti
1 cup diced cooked chicken (or 1 jar [5½ ounces] canned chicken, diced)
1 cup diced cooked ham
¼ cup sliced, pitted ripe olives
¼ cup minced parsley
1 teaspoon grated orange rind
1 teaspoon salt
¼ teaspoon freshly ground pepper
1 cup dairy sour cream
½ cup milk
¼ cup breadcrumbs
2 tablespoons grated Parmesan cheese

Cook spaghetti in boiling salted water until tender, about 7 minutes. Drain. Combine chicken, ham, olives, parsley, orange rind, salt, pepper and spaghetti. Mix lightly. Blend sour cream with milk. Toss lightly with spaghetti mixture. Pour into a buttered 2-quart casserole. Mix breadcrumbs with Parmesan cheese and sprinkle on top. Bake in a 350° F. oven for 30 minutes or until hot and bubbly. Garnish with additional olives and parsley if desired. This casserole can be prepared in advance, refrigerated and baked at serving time. Add 15 minutes to baking time. Refrigerate mixture in a covered bowl and spoon into casserole just before baking.

Makes 4 servings.

CHICKEN DIVINE

2 (2½ to 3 pounds) broiler-fryer chickens
1 clove garlic
1 cup dairy sour cream
2 tablespoons lemon juice
1 teaspoon seasoned salt
1 teaspoon salt
1 teaspoon paprika
Dash Tabasco
1 cup fine dry breadcrumbs
½ cup butter, melted

Disjoint chicken using only meaty pieces. (Save wings, necks, giblets and back for broth.) Wash and dry chicken. Mash garlic and mix with sour cream, lemon juice and seasonings. Coat chicken with sour cream mixture. Let stand, covered, several hours or overnight in refrigerator. Butter a large shallow casserole. Remove chicken pieces carefully from cream and gently roll in crumbs. Arrange in a single layer in casserole. Drizzle butter over chicken. Bake in a 350° F. oven for 50 to 60 minutes or until chicken is tender and golden brown.

Makes 4 to 6 servings.

CHICKEN MARCONI

3½- to 4-pound chicken, cut up
¼ cup flour
3 tablespoons olive oil
½ cup chopped onion
1 clove garlic, finely chopped
½ cup chopped celery
1 can (3 ounces) sliced mushrooms and liquid
¼ cup chopped parsley
2 cups chicken broth
1 can (6 ounces) tomato paste
½ teaspoon salt
1 teaspoon dried rosemary
¼ teaspoon freshly ground pepper

Cut up chicken and use neck, giblets and backs for chicken broth. Wash and dry remaining pieces and coat with flour. Heat oil in large skillet and brown chicken on all sides. Transfer chicken pieces to shallow 2-quart casserole. Lightly brown onion, garlic and celery in skillet. Add remaining ingredients to onion mixture in skillet. Cook and scrape brown crust from bottom of skillet. Simmer 5 minutes, uncovered. Pour over chicken in casserole. Cover and bake in a 350° F. oven for 30 minutes. Uncover and bake 30 minutes longer.

Makes 4 servings.

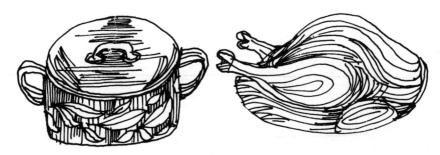

COQ AU VIN

2 (2½ pounds each) frying chickens, disjointed
2 teaspoons salt
¼ teaspoon freshly ground pepper
3 tablespoons flour
6 tablespoons butter
16 small whole onions
4 shallots, minced
¼ cup chopped onion
2 cloves garlic, minced
16 mushroom caps
2 cups dry red wine
½ teaspoon thyme
1 bay leaf

Disjoint chicken and save backs for broth. Wash and dry remaining pieces. Mix salt, pepper and flour and rub into chicken pieces. Heat butter in large skillet and brown the chicken. Transfer to casserole. Add whole onions, shallots, minced onions, garlic and mushrooms to skillet and cook and stir over low heat until onions are lightly browned. Spoon over chicken in casserole. Add wine to skillet and heat and scrape brown crust from skillet. Pour wine, thyme and bay leaf over chicken. Cover and bake in a 350° F. oven for 1 hour or until chicken is tender.

Makes 4 to 6 servings.

SWEET-SOUR DUCKLING

1 4- to 5-pound ready-to-cook duckling, quartered
1 can (13 ounces) pineapple chunks
⅓ cup soy sauce
3 tablespoons brown sugar
1 teaspoon salt
1 clove garlic, mashed
1 cup water
½ teaspoon salt
2 tablespoons soy sauce
1 teaspoon salt
1½ cups chopped green pepper
2 green onions, chopped
3 tablespoons brown sugar
2 tablespoons cornstarch
¼ cup water

Rinse duckling and pat dry. Put into shallow casserole. Drain pineapple juice. Measure ⅓ cup and combine with ⅓ cup soy sauce, 3 tablespoons brown sugar, 1 teaspoon salt and garlic. Pour over duckling. Bake in a 325° F. oven for about 2 hours, basting occasionally. While duck is cooking, simmer giblets in water with ½ teaspoon salt, covered, until tender. Pour duck broth into saucepan and add remaining pineapple juice, pineapple chunks, 2 tablespoons soy sauce, 1 teaspoon salt, green pepper, green onion and 3 tablespoons brown sugar. Cook 5 minutes. Mix cornstarch with ¼ cup water. Stir into hot mixture. Cook and stir until thickened and clear. Serve with roast duckling.

Makes 4 servings.

CORNISH GAME HENS EDERRA

2 Cornish game hens
¼ teaspoon salt
Dash freshly ground pepper
3 slices bacon
1 cup soft white breadcrumbs
1 tablespoon chopped onion
1 small garlic clove, chopped
¼ tcaspoon salt
Pinch thyme
Livers from hens, chopped
⅓ cup olive oil
4 apples, peeled and sliced
¼ cup cream

Wash and dry hens and rub cavity with ¼ teaspoon salt and pepper. Cut bacon into 2-inch pieces and fry until partially done. Remove bacon and reserve. To bacon fat, add breadcrumbs, onion, garlic, ¼ teaspoon salt, thyme, and livers. Toss together and cook over low heat, stirring until blended and lightly toasted. Stuff hens with mixture and truss. Heat olive oil in skillet and brown hens on all sides. Keep skillet partially covered to prevent spattering. Transfer browned hens to small casserole and spoon apples and bacon around them. Cover and bake in a 350° F. oven for about 40 minutes or until tender. Stir in cream, remove trussing and serve.

Makes 2 servings.

TIP: Tiny peas and mushrooms go well with this dish.

TURKEY NAVARESE

1 6-pound turkey
¼ cup diced salt pork
¼ cup olive oil
1 teaspoon salt
2 cups tomato sauce
2 cups dry white wine
8 white onions, peeled
8 chestnuts, peeled
2 carrots, cut in pieces
¼ cup diced, spicy Italian sausage

Have butcher cut turkey in pieces and remove bone from breast. Cut breast in two pieces. (Save back and breast bone for broth.) Fry salt pork on medium heat until crisp. Remove from skillet and reserve. Brown turkey pieces and transfer to a buttered 2½-quart casserole as browned. Mix remaining ingredients and add to turkey in casserole. Cover and bake at 350° F. for 1½ hours or until tender. Sprinkle with salt pork.

Makes 8 servings.

TURKEY CLUB CASSEROLE

2 cups chopped, cooked boneless turkey roast
1 can (10½ ounces) condensed cream-of-chicken soup
¼ teaspoon garlic salt
⅛ teaspoon ground rosemary
Dash white pepper
1 cup smooth cottage cheese
1 package (10 ounces) frozen chopped spinach, cooked
    and drained
2 cups cooked wide egg noodles
¾ cup (6 ounces) shredded mozzarella cheese
Paprika

Mix turkey, soup and seasonings. Mix together cottage cheese and spinach. In a buttered 2-quart casserole, alternately layer half the noodles, turkey and cottage-cheese mixtures. Sprinkle with half the mozzarella cheese. Repeat. Bake in a 350° F. oven for 40 minutes or until top is bubbling and lightly browned. Sprinkle with paprika. Let stand 10 minutes for easier serving. This casserole can be prepared in advance, refrigerated and baked at serving time. Add another 15 minutes baking time.

Makes 6 servings.

TURKEY LOUISE

½ cup sliced onion
½ cup chopped green pepper
2 tablespoons butter
1 can (1 pound 4 ounces) pineapple tidbits
1¼ cups turkey or chicken broth
2 tablespoons cornstarch
1½ teaspoons salt
1 teaspoon curry powder
3 cups toasted ½-inch bread cubes
1½ cups chopped cooked turkey or chicken
¼ cup slivered almonds

Cook onion and green pepper in butter until tender. Drain pineapple tidbits and add turkey broth to juice to make 2 cups. Dissolve cornstarch, salt, and curry in liquid and add to cooked onions. Cook and stir until sauce boils and is thickened. Arrange half of bread cubes, turkey, pineapple and almonds in layers in a buttered 1½-quart casserole, ending with bread cubes, and pour half of sauce over. Repeat. Bake in a 350° F. oven for 30 minutes.

Makes 4 servings.

CRABMEAT IMPERIAL

4 tablespoons butter
1 tablespoon chopped green pepper
¼ teaspoon dry mustard
¼ teaspoon paprika
½ teaspoon salt
4 tablespoons flour
1 cup milk
2 teaspoons capers
1 teaspoon Worcestershire sauce
1 pound crabmeat
1 egg yolk
6 tablespoons mayonnaise

Heat butter and sauté green pepper 2 minutes. Add mustard, paprika, salt and flour and let bubble. Stir in milk and cook and stir until mixture comes to a boil and is thickened. Fold in capers and Worcestershire sauce. Shred crabmeat and remove any spines. Add with egg yolk and mayonnaise to sauce. Spoon into 4 individual buttered casseroles or a buttered shallow casserole. Bake in a 400° F. oven 20 minutes for the individuals, 25 to 30 minutes for the large casserole.

Makes 4 servings.

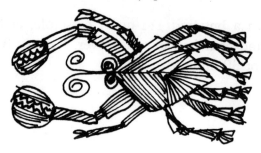

CRAB CRÊPES

1 recipe crêpes (p. 119)
¼ cup butter
1 cup chopped mushrooms
¼ cup flour
Dash cayenne
1 cup fish stock
½ cup cream
2 egg yolks, beaten
2 tablespoons white wine
½ teaspoon salt
Freshly ground pepper to taste
1 pound crabmeat
3 tablespoons Parmesan cheese

Prepare crêpes in advance. Melt butter over low heat and sauté mushrooms for 5 minutes. Stir in flour and let bubble. Add cayenne and fish stock and cook and stir until mixture boils. Mix cream with egg yolks and stir into hot mixture. Add wine, salt, and pepper. Remove spines from crabmeat and mix with about ⅔ of sauce. Place in center of pancakes. Roll pancakes around filling and arrange in a buttered shallow casserole. Spoon remainder of sauce over top of pancakes and sprinkle with Parmesan cheese. Bake in a 425° F. oven for 15 minutes or until nicely browned.

Makes 4 servings.

ANNE'S DEVILED CRAB

12 hard-shelled crabs or 1 can (13 ounces) crabmeat
4 tablespoons butter
2 tablespoons flour
1 tablespoon chopped parsley
2 teaspoons lemon juice
1 teaspoon prepared mustard
½ teaspoon bottled horseradish
1 teaspoon salt
1 cup milk
2 hard-cooked eggs, shelled and chopped
½ cup soft breadcrumbs
2 tablespoons melted butter

If hard-shelled crabs are used, cook in boiling water for about 5 minutes. Cool at once by plunging in cold water. Drain and pick out crabmeat, discarding spines. Reserve 6 of the upper shells. If canned crabmeat is used, drain and remove all spines. Melt 4 tablespoons of butter in saucepan over low heat. Add flour and let bubble. Then stir in parsley, lemon juice, mustard, horseradish, salt and milk. Cook and stir until mixture boils and is thickened. Add crabmeat and chopped eggs. Spoon into crab shells or 6 individual ramekins or casseroles. Mix breadcrumbs with melted butter and sprinkle over crabmeat. Bake in a 400° F. oven for 10 minutes or until thoroughly heated. This casserole can be prepared in advance, refrigerated and baked at serving time. Add 10 minutes to cooking time.

Makes 6 servings.

CRAB CHEESE CASSEROLE

2½ cups medium noodles (5-ounce package)
2 tablespoons minced onion
½ cup finely diced celery
¼ cup butter
¼ cup flour
½ teaspoon mustard
1 teaspoon salt
2 cups milk
1 tablespoon lemon juice
1 can (7½ ounces) crabmeat
2 cups creamed cottage cheese (16 ounces)
½ cup buttered crumbs

Cook noodles in boiling salted water only until tender. Drain and rinse thoroughly with cold water and drain again. Cook onion and celery in butter in saucepan until tender but not browned. Stir in flour, mustard and salt and cook until bubbly. Slowly add milk and cook and stir until mixture boils and is thickened. Stir in lemon juice. Remove any spines from crabmeat. Mix together noodles, sauce, crabmeat and cottage cheese. Pour into buttered 2-quart casserole and sprinkle

crumbs over the top. Bake in a 350° F. oven for 30 to 40 minutes. This casserole can be prepared in advance, refrigerated and heated at serving time. Add 15 minutes to cooking time.

Makes 4 servings.

SCALLOPS IN WHITE WINE

1½ pounds scallops
4 tablespoons butter
½ pound fresh mushrooms, sliced
¼ cup finely chopped onion
2 tablespoons flour
1 cup dry white wine
2 teaspoons lemon juice
1 teaspoon salt
Freshly ground pepper to taste
2 tablespoons parsley
1 cup buttered crumbs
Paprika

Wash and dry scallops and, if large, cut in two. Heat butter in skillet and sauté mushrooms and onions until tender. Stir in flour and cook several minutes. Stir in wine, lemon juice, salt, pepper and parsley and bring to a boil. Add scallops. Spoon into one large shallow casserole or six individual casseroles. Sprinkle with buttered crumbs and paprika. Bake in a 400° F. oven—25 minutes for large casserole, 15 minutes for individuals.

Makes 6 servings.

SCALLOPS AND CRAB DIABLE

4 tablespoons butter
1 package (12 ounces) frozen scallops, defrosted (or
        1 pound fresh scallops)
⅓ cup flour
2 cups milk
¼ cup finely chopped pimiento
2 tablespoons Worcestershire sauce
1 tablespoon Dijon-style mustard
1 teaspoon salt
1 teaspoon dry mustard
½ teaspoon Tabasco
⅛ teaspoon freshly ground pepper
1 package (6 or 8 ounces) frozen cooked crabmeat (or
        1 can [7½ ounces] king crab)
4 hard-cooked eggs, chopped
½ cup soft breadcrumbs
2 tablespoons melted butter

Heat 4 tablespoons butter in saucepan and cook scallops for several minutes. Remove and reserve. Stir flour into butter and cook until bubbly. Gradually stir in milk and cook and stir until mixture boils and is thickened. Stir in pimiento and seasonings. Remove any spines from crab. Combine scallops, crabmeat and eggs in cream sauce. Pour into buttered 1½-quart casserole. Mix breadcrumbs with melted butter and sprinkle on seafood mixture in casserole. Bake in a 450° F. oven for 20 minutes. This casserole can be prepared in advance, refrigerated and baked at serving time. Add 15 minutes to cooking time.

Makes 6 servings.

LOBSTER SOUFFLÉ

3 tablespoons butter
4 tablespoons flour
1 cup chicken broth
1 cup light cream
1 teaspoon salt
Dash Tabasco
1 tablespoon minced parsley
½ cup fine dry breadcrumbs
2 cups cooked lobster meat, diced fine
4 eggs

Heat butter, add flour and let bubble. Stir in chicken broth and cream and cook and stir until mixture comes to a boil and is thickened. Remove from heat. Add salt and pepper, parsley, breadcrumbs and lobster meat. Beat egg whites until very stiff. Beat egg yolks until thick and lemon-colored and fold into lobster mixture. Fold in egg whites. Pour into a 2-quart soufflé dish or casserole of similar shape. Bake in a 325° F. oven for about 1 hour. Serve immediately with mushroom sauce (p. 223).

Makes 4 to 6 servings.

SCALLOPED OYSTERS

¾ cup melted butter
3 cups toasted breadcrumbs
1 teaspoon salt
⅛ teaspoon freshly ground pepper
¼ teaspoon nutmeg
1½ pints oysters
⅓ cup oyster liquor
⅓ cup cream
Paprika

Mix butter with breadcrumbs and seasonings. Drain oysters, reserving ⅓ cup liquor. In a buttered shallow casserole, put in a layer of half the oysters and top it with half the crumbs. Repeat and pour the oyster liquor and cream over the casserole. Sprinkle with paprika. Bake in a 375° F. oven for 25 to 30 minutes or until browned.

Makes 4 to 6 servings.

SHRIMP DE JONGHE

2 pounds raw shrimp
1 cup dry breadcrumbs
½ cup butter, melted
¼ cup chopped green onions
2 cloves garlic, finely chopped
2 tablespoons finely chopped parsley
1 teaspoon chervil
1 teaspoon tarragon vinegar
1 teaspoon thyme
½ cup sherry
1 teaspoon salt
Freshly ground pepper to taste
2 tablespoons butter, melted
½ cup dry breadcrumbs

Peel, devein and wash shrimp. Dry well. Combine 1 cup crumbs with ½ cup butter, onion, garlic, parsley, chervil, vinegar, thyme, sherry, salt and pepper. Place alternate layers of shrimp and crumb mixture in a buttered 1½-quart casserole. Combine 2 tablespoons butter with ½ cup crumbs and sprinkle over top of casserole. Bake in a 350° F. oven for 1 hour or until nicely browned.

Makes 6 servings.

AMERICAN SPAGHETTI SHRIMP CURRY

1 package (8 ounces) elbow spaghetti
1 teaspoon salt
2 teaspoons curry powder
¼ teaspoon freshly ground pepper
⅛ teaspoon ginger
½ cup white seedless raisins
½ cup flaked coconut
½ cup chopped walnuts
½ cup chopped onions
½ cup chopped apple
1 pound raw shrimp, cooked, cleaned and chopped
1 can (10½ ounces) cream-of-celery soup
¾ cup water

Cook spaghetti in boiling salted water until tender, about 7 minutes. Drain. Add salt, curry powder, pepper, ginger, raisins, coconut, walnuts, onion, apple and shrimp. Toss lightly to mix. Blend soup with water and stir carefully into spaghetti mixture. Pour into buttered flat 2-quart casserole and bake in a 350° F. oven 25 to 30 minutes or until lightly browned and bubbly. This casserole can be partially prepared in advance. Mix cooked spaghetti with seasonings and shrimp, then refrigerate. When ready to bake, stir in soup and water. Add 15 minutes to baking time.

Makes 4 servings.

CIOPPINO KEY WEST

¼ cup chopped onion
2 tablespoons olive oil
2 cups clam broth
2 cups peeled and chopped ripe tomatoes
1 carrot finely chopped
1 cup chopped celery
½ teaspoon salt
¼ teaspoon dry mustard
½ teaspoon paprika
¼ teaspoon oregano
1 clove garlic, chopped
2 bay leaves
½ pound raw shrimp, shelled and deveined
½ pound scallops
½ pint oysters
1 can (6½ ounces) crabmeat
1 pound fillet of sole or haddock
Melted butter
Parmesan cheese

In a large casserole, sauté onion in oil until golden. Add clam broth, tomatoes, carrot, celery and seasonings. Cover and simmer 1 hour, stirring occasionally. Add shrimp and scallops and cook 10 minutes longer. Stir in oysters and crabmeat. Meanwhile, cut fish fillet into 6 pieces and brush with melted butter. Broil until almost done (about 6 minutes). Sprinkle with Parmesan cheese and broil 2 to 3 minutes longer. Place fillets into seafood mixture and serve in bowls.

Makes 6 servings.

BAKED HALIBUT CREOLE

2 pounds halibut steaks
⅔ cup thinly sliced onion
1½ cups chopped fresh mushrooms
⅓ cup chopped, peeled tomato
¼ cup chopped green pepper
¼ cup chopped parsley
3 tablespoons chopped pimiento
½ cup dry white wine
2 tablespoons lemon juice
1 teaspoon salt
¼ teaspoon dill weed
Freshly ground pepper

Wipe fish with paper towel and cut into serving-size portions. Arrange onion slices in bottom of buttered shallow casserole and place fish steaks on onion slices. Mix mushrooms with tomatoes, green pepper, parsley and pimiento and spread over fish. Combine wine with remaining ingredients and pour over casserole. Bake in a 350° F. oven for 30 minutes or until fish flakes easily when tested with a fork.

Makes 6 servings.

FISH CASSEROLE MARGUERY

1½ pounds fillet of sole, flounder or haddock
4 tablespoons finely chopped onion
1 can (10½ ounces) cream-of-mushroom soup
1 can (4½ ounces) tiny shrimp, drained
½ teaspoon paprika

Arrange serving-size pieces of fish in a buttered flat casserole. Mix onion with soup and shrimp and spoon over fish. Sprinkle with paprika. Bake in a 400° F. oven for 30 minutes or until fish can be flaked with a fork.

Makes 4 servings.

NEW ENGLAND CODFISH PIE

Filling:
½ pound salt codfish, cut up
¼ pound lean salt pork
½ cup chopped onion
3 tablespoons flour
⅛ teaspoon freshly ground pepper
2½ cups milk
1 cup diced, cooked potatoes
Biscuit dough:
1 cup flour, sifted
1½ teaspoons baking powder
½ teaspoon salt
2 tablespoons shortening
⅓ cup (approximately) milk

Soak codfish in water 2 hours, changing water 3 times. Cover with fresh water and simmer until it is tender and can be shredded (about 10 minutes). Drain. Cook salt pork in frying pan until crisp. Remove salt pork and all but 3 tablespoons of fat. Cook onion until tender but not browned. Blend in flour and pepper and let bubble. Gradually stir in milk and cook and stir until mixture boils and is thickened. Add codfish, salt pork and potatoes. Pour mixture into buttered 1½-quart baking dish.

Sift flour, baking powder and salt together. Cut in shortening with pastry blender or two knives until texture of cornmeal. Stir in milk until flour is moistened. Pat out ½-inch thick on lightly floured board and with a biscuit cutter cut into biscuits. Put biscuits on top of fish mixture in casserole. Bake in a 450° F. oven 15 minutes or until hot and biscuits browned.

Makes 4 servings.

BAKED CHOWDER

1 pound finnan haddie
Cold water
¼ cup diced salt pork
1 cup chopped onion
2 cups diced raw potato
½ teaspoon salt
Dash freshly ground pepper
1 quart milk
2 tablespoons chopped parsley

Cover finnan haddie with cold water and soak for 1 hour. Cook salt pork until crisp, add onion and continue cooking until tender but not browned. Drain fish and transfer to a buttered 2-quart baking dish. Spoon salt pork, onion, potato and seasonings over finnan haddie. Heat milk to boiling and pour over finnan haddie in casserole. Cover and bake in a 350° F. oven for 45 minutes or until potatoes are tender. Before serving, flake finnan haddie. Serve in bowls.

Makes 4 servings.

BASIC CHEESE SOUFFLÉ

6 tablespoons butter
8 tablespoons flour
1 teaspoon salt
¼ teaspoon freshly ground pepper
2 cups milk
1½ cups (about ¼ pound) shredded natural sharp
    Cheddar cheese
Dash cayenne
4 eggs, separated

Heat butter in saucepan. Add flour, salt and pepper and let bubble. Stir in milk and cook and stir until mixture comes to a boil and is thickened. Remove from heat and stir in cheese and cayenne. Stir until cheese melts. Beat egg whites until very stiff. Beat egg yolks until thick and lemon-colored. Fold into cheese sauce. Fold in egg whites. Pour into a 1½-quart soufflé dish or casserole of similar shape. Bake in a 425° F. oven 25 minutes. Serve immediately with crisp bacon or mushroom sauce.

Makes 3 to 4 servings.

VARIATIONS:

1. *Cheese-Ham Soufflé:* Follow recipe for Cheese Soufflé. Fold ½ cup ground ham into sauce with cheese.
2. *Cheese-Mushroom Soufflé:* Follow recipe for Cheese Soufflé. Sauté 1 cup finely chopped mushrooms in 1 tablespoon butter. Season with salt and pepper and fold into soufflé mixture with egg whites.
3. *Cheese-Shrimp Soufflé:* Follow recipe for Cheese Soufflé. Drain 1 can (4½ ounces) shrimp and chop very fine. Fold into sauce with cheese.

Mushroom Sauce:
3 tablespoons butter
1 cup sliced mushrooms
2 tablespoons flour
¼ teaspoon salt
Dash Tabasco
1¼ cups milk

Heat butter in saucepan and sauté mushrooms until tender. Stir in flour and seasonings and let bubble. Stir in milk and cook and stir until mixture comes to a boil and is thickened.

Makes 1½ cups.

Notes on Making Soufflés:

Soufflés are not nearly as tricky as their reputation would indicate. The cheese sauce can be any temperature without causing disaster, but warm is best. Beat both egg yolks and whites thoroughly. (I've suggested beating the egg whites before the yolks so that you will not have to wash the eggbeater in-between.) Once the egg whites are beaten very stiff, proceed immediately with the rest of the recipe. To make a top hat on your soufflé, cut through the batter with a spatula in a circle parallel to edge of pan and in about an inch from the edge.

The soufflé can be baked in a 325° F. oven for about 1 hour if the longer time is more convenient. But whichever way you bake it, be sure your guests are ready to eat when the soufflé comes out of the oven. That is the one part that *is* tricky. It won't wait very gracefully.

EASY CHEESE SOUFFLÉ

1 can (10½ ounces) condensed cream-of-mushroom
    soup
2 cups shredded natural Cheddar cheese
6 eggs, separated

Heat mushroom soup with cheese over low heat, stirring until cheese is melted. Beat egg whites until very stiff. Beat egg yolks until thick and lemon-colored. Fold soup-cheese mixture into egg yolks, mixing thoroughly. Then fold in egg whites. Pour into buttered 2-quart casserole. Bake in a 400° F. oven for 30 minutes. Serve at once. For comments on soufflé preparation see p. 223.

Makes 4 servings.

MOZZARELLA SPINACH AMERICANA

8 slices bread, crusts removed
8 slices (1 ounce each) mozzarella cheese
1 package (10 ounces) frozen chopped spinach
¼ cup pizza sauce
2 cups milk
½ teaspoon salt
3 eggs, beaten
¼ teaspoon paprika

Place 4 bread slices in a square 9-inch casserole. Arrange 4 slices of cheese over bread. Cook spinach in a small amount of salted water until thawed. Drain and spread over cheese slices. Top with pizza sauce, remaining bread and cheese slices. Combine milk and salt with beaten eggs; pour over sandwiches. Sprinkle paprika over top. Bake in a 350° F. oven about 45 minutes or until browned. This casserole can be prepared in advance, refrigerated and baked at serving time. Add 15 minutes to baking time.

Makes 4 servings.

SPINACH CASSEROLE

- 2 packages (10 ounces each) frozen spinach, cooked and drained
- 2 cups cooked noodles
- 1 cup shredded processed American cheese
- 1 can (10½ ounces) condensed cream-of-mushroom soup
- ⅓ cup milk
- ⅛ teaspoon ground nutmeg

Arrange layers of spinach, noodles, and ¾ cup of the cheese in buttered 1½-quart casserole. Blend soup with milk and nutmeg and pour over noodle spinach mixture. Top with remaining cheese. Bake in a 375° F. oven 45 minutes.

Makes 4 servings.

CHAMPIGNONS GRUYERE

½ pound fresh mushrooms
1 tablespoon lemon juice
¼ teaspoon salt
Freshly ground pepper to taste
¼ cup butter
¼ cup all-purpose flour
2 cups milk
½ teaspoon salt
Freshly ground pepper to taste
1 cup shredded natural Gruyere or Swiss cheese
½ cup butter
1 cup boiling water
1 cup all-purpose flour
½ teaspoon salt
4 eggs

Remove stems from mushroom caps and chop. Wash caps, dry and dip in lemon juice, mixed with ¼ teaspoon salt and pepper. Place caps in buttered shallow casserole. Sauté chopped mushrooms in ¼ cup butter for 2 to 3 minutes. Stir in flour and let bubble. Gradually add milk and cook and stir until mixture boils and is thickened. Add ½ teaspoon salt, pepper and ⅓ cup of cheese. Cover and keep warm.

To make dumplings: Bring ½ cup butter and water to a boil, add 1 cup flour and stir over low heat until mixture leaves sides of pan. Remove from heat. Add eggs, one at a time, beating after each addition until mixture is smooth and glossy. Stir in ¼ cup of the cheese. Drop by rounded teaspoonfuls into boiling salted water and cook until dumplings rise to the top, 2 to 3 minutes. Drain. Place dumplings on mushrooms in casserole. Cover with cheese sauce and sprinkle with remaining cheese. Bake in a 375° F. oven 20 to 25 minutes or until cheese is lightly browned. Serve at once.

Makes 4 to 6 servings.

RIPE OLIVE BAKE

2 packages (10 ounces each) frozen broccoli spears
Butter
6 slices day-old bread
¾ cup pitted California ripe olives
1 cup shredded American processed cheese
4 eggs
2 cups milk
1 teaspoon salt
⅛ teaspoon freshly ground pepper
Dash nutmeg

Cook broccoli according to package directions only until tender-crisp. Drain and arrange in 6 individual casseroles. Butter both sides of bread and cut into cubes and place over broccoli. Sprinkle with ripe olives cut into wedges and cheese. Beat eggs with milk and seasonings and pour over casseroles. Bake in a 350° F. oven 30 minutes or until custard is set.

Makes 6 servings.

THREE-LAYERED NOODLES

1 package (8 ounces) wide noodles
2 tablespoons cooking oil
2 cups smooth cottage cheese
2 cups dairy sour cream
2 tablespoons butter
1 clove garlic, finely chopped
¾ cup finely chopped onion
¾ pound ground-beef chuck
1 can (6 ounces) tomato paste
1 bay leaf
1 teaspoon salt
⅛ teaspoon freshly ground pepper

Cook noodles according to package directions. Drain, mix with oil and pour into buttered 2-quart casserole. Mix cottage cheese and sour cream and pour over noodles. Heat butter in skillet and cook garlic, onion, and beef until lightly browned. Add tomato paste, bay leaf, salt and pepper and mix well. Spoon over mixture in casserole. Bake in a 350° F. oven for 30 minutes or until bubbly.

Makes 4 servings.

NOODLE CHEESE CASSEROLE

1 package (12 ounces) medium noodles
2 tablespoons salad oil
½ cup chopped onion
2 tablespoons Worcestershire sauce
¼ cup chopped fresh parsley
½ teaspoon salt
⅛ teaspoon Tabasco
2 cups sour cream
2 cups smooth cottage cheese
½ cup buttered fine breadcrumbs

Cook noodles as directed until just tender. Drain and mix with salad oil. Combine remaining ingredients except

breadcrumbs and arrange in alternate layers with noodles in a buttered 2-quart casserole. Sprinkle top with breadcrumbs. Bake in a 350° F. oven 20 to 25 minutes or until bubbly.

Makes 6 servings.

LASAGNE

½ cup chopped onion
1 clove garlic, minced
2 tablespoons olive oil
1 pound ground-beef chuck
1 can (8 ounces) tomato sauce
1 can (6 ounces) tomato paste
1 cup water
½ teaspoon oregano
Freshly ground pepper to taste
1 teaspoon salt
½ teaspoon basil
1 whole clove, crushed
8 ounces lasagne noodles, cooked *al dente,* drained
2 cups ricotta or cottage cheese
½ cup shredded Parmesan cheese
8 ounces sliced mozzarella cheese

Sauté onion and garlic in oil until tender. Add meat and brown. Add tomato sauce and paste, water and seasonings and simmer, covered, 20 to 30 minutes. Place half of lasagne in bottom of buttered shallow 13x9-inch casserole. Spread half of ricotta, Parmesan, and mozzarella cheese over lasagne. Add half to meat sauce. Repeat layers. Bake in a 350° F. oven 45 minutes.

Makes 6 servings.

ZUCCHINI MADISON

4 large (about 2½ pounds) zucchini squash
1 pound ground beef-chuck
½ cup chopped onion
1 teaspoon salt
¼ teaspoon freshly ground pepper
¼ teaspoon chili powder
2 cups toasted bread cubes, ½ inch
1 cup shredded sharp Cheddar cheese
2 cans (8 ounces each) tomato sauce
½ cup water

Wash and peel zucchini. Dice half of the zucchini and slice the remainder. Brown beef and onion and add seasonings. Mix with bread cubes, diced zucchini, ½ cup cheese and 1 can tomato sauce. Spoon mixture into buttered 1½-quart casserole. Arrange sliced zucchini on top and sprinkle with remaining cheese. Mix the other can of tomato sauce with water and pour over the casserole. Cover and bake in a 350° F. oven for 45 minutes. Uncover and continue baking until zucchini is tender, about 15 minutes longer.

Makes 6 servings.

ZUCCHINI SAN MATEO

4 medium zucchini (about 1½ pounds)
Salt
2 tablespoons grated Parmesan cheese
1 jar (7 ounces) pimiento pods, well drained
6 thin slices salami
6 ounces natural Swiss cheese, cut in 6 portions
1 cup saltine cracker crumbs
¼ cup chopped parsley
⅓ cup butter or margarine, melted

Wash zucchini, cut off stem ends and cut in thirds lengthwise. Sprinkle lightly with salt and let stand 15 minutes. Pat dry with paper towels. Arrange in two layers in a buttered 2-quart rectangular casserole. Sprinkle Parmesan cheese over each layer. Split pimiento pods along one side and lay flat. Place a slice of salami and a portion of cheese on each. Roll up and arrange on top of zucchini. Combine crumbs with parsley and butter and sprinkle over casserole. Cover and bake in a 350° F. oven for 45 minutes. Uncover and bake 10 to 15 minutes longer.

Makes 6 servings.

CHRIS'S WILD-RICE CASSEROLE

2 cups boiling water
⅔ cup wild rice
1 can (10¾ ounces) chicken-rice soup
1 can (4 ounces) sliced mushrooms
½ cup water
1 teaspoon salt
⅛ teaspoon celery salt
⅛ teaspoon onion salt
⅛ teaspoon garlic salt
⅛ teaspoon paprika
⅛ teaspoon liquid smoke
1 small bay leaf, crumbled
3 tablespoons chopped onion
3 tablespoons oil
1 pound ground beef-chuck

Pour boiling water over wild rice. Cover and let stand 15 minutes. Drain. Add soup, mushrooms and liquid, ½ cup water and seasonings. Sauté onion in oil until lightly browned. Add ground beef and cook until lightly browned, breaking into small pieces with fork. Mix onion and beef with rice mixture. Spoon into buttered 2-quart casserole and bake in a 325° F. oven for 1 hour. This casserole may be prepared in advance, refrigerated and baked at serving time. Add 15 minutes to baking time.

Makes 4 servings.

QUICK RICE CASSEROLE

5 slices bacon, diced
½ cup diced celery
1 can (4 ounces) sliced mushrooms
Water
1 cup canned tomatoes
1 envelope (1⅜ ounces) dehydrated onion-soup mix
1⅓ cups precooked rice
¾ cup shredded Cheddar cheese

Fry bacon until crisp. Pour off all except 2 tablespoons drippings. Add celery to drippings and sauté until tender. Drain and measure mushroom liquid and add water to make 1½ cups. Mix with tomatoes, onion soup, rice and ½ cup cheese in buttered 1½-quart casserole. Stir in mushrooms, celery and bacon. Top with remaining cheese. Cover and bake in a 375° F. oven for 20 minutes or until rice is tender.

Makes 4 servings.

VEGETABLES AND OTHER CASSEROLES TO GO WITH

Here you will find a variety of recipes that can be served with grilled meats or oven-baked meats, such as ham, beef, turkey or the ubiquitous meat loaf. Since those casseroles are taking up cupboard space, one should use them in as many ways as possible. And these "go withs" will be just what you need to round out the meal on many occasions.

POTATOES GOTHENBURG

4 tablespoons butter
2 cups sliced onion
4 medium potatoes
1 can (2 ounces) flat anchovy fillets
½ teaspoon salt
¼ teaspoon freshly ground pepper
1 tablespoon toasted breadcrumbs
1½ cups evaporated milk

Heat 2 tablespoons butter in skillet and sauté onions until tender but not browned. Peel potatoes and slice thin, then

233

into narrow strips. Arrange cooked onions in buttered 1½-quart casserole. Layer anchovy fillets (reserve liquid) on top of onions and add potatoes. Sprinkle with salt, pepper and breadcrumbs and dot with remaining butter. Bake in a 425° F. oven 20 minutes. Pour evaporated milk and reserved anchovy liquid over potatoes and continue baking 25 minutes longer or until tender.

Makes 6 servings.

BAKED CREAMED POTATOES

3 tablespoons butter
2 tablespoons flour
1 teaspoon salt
¼ teaspoon freshly ground pepper
2 cups milk
4 cups thinly sliced peeled potatoes
1 cup finely chopped onion
1 teaspoon salt
3 tablespoons chopped parsley

Heat butter, add flour, 1 teaspoon salt and pepper and let bubble. Stir in milk and cook and stir until mixture comes to a boil and is thickened. Combine potatoes, onion, 1 teaspoon salt in saucepan. Add boiling water an inch deep. Cover and simmer 10 minutes. Drain. Spread half the potatoes in buttered 1½-quart casserole. Add half the sauce, sprinkle with half the parsley. Repeat. Bake in a 350° F. oven 45 minutes or until tender and browned.

Makes 4 to 6 servings.

CHEESE SOUFFLÉED POTATOES

¼ cup chopped green pepper
¼ cup chopped green onion
2 tablespoons butter
Instant mashed potatoes for 4 servings
⅓ cup milk
4 eggs, separated
½ teaspoon salt
⅛ teaspoon freshly ground pepper
½ cup shredded processed American cheese

Cook green pepper and onion in butter until tender but not brown. Prepare instant potatoes for 4 servings, as directed on package, adding ⅓ cup more milk. Beat in egg yolks one at a time. Add cooked pepper and onion, salt and pepper. Beat egg whites until stiff and fold in potato mixture. Pour into a buttered 10x6x2-inch casserole. Bake in a 350° F. oven for 35 minutes or until done. Quickly sprinkle shredded cheese over the top. Cut into squares and serve at once.

Makes 4 to 6 servings.

SUPERB POTATO SCALLOP

3 cups sliced cooked potatoes
1 cup dairy sour cream
2 eggs, slightly beaten
¼ cup milk
¼ cup chopped frozen chives
½ teaspoon salt
Dash freshly ground pepper
1 cup shredded sharp American cheese

Arrange potatoes in buttered shallow 1½-quart casserole. Mix sour cream with eggs, milk and seasonings. Pour over potatoes. Cover with cheese. Bake in a 350° F. oven 30 minutes until heated through and delicately browned.

Makes 4 servings.

BAKED POTATO SALAD

8 slices bacon
½ cup chopped onion
⅓ cup vinegar
1 teaspoon salt
¼ teaspoon freshly ground pepper
1 tablespoon sugar
3 cups sliced cooked potatoes
½ cup chopped green pepper
½ cup chopped pimiento

Cook bacon until crisp. Drain on paper towels. Break into pieces. Measure 6 tablespoons bacon fat in skillet. Add onion, vinegar, salt, pepper and sugar and bring to a boil. Lightly stir remaining ingredients, including bacon, into hot vinegar mixture. Spoon into a buttered 1-quart casserole. Bake, uncovered, in a 375° F. oven for 20 minutes. This casserole can be prepared in advance, refrigerated and baked at serving time. Toss potatoes in casserole with a fork just before putting in oven. Add 10 to 15 minutes to baking time.

Makes 4 to 6 servings.

CURRIED POTATO AND ONION CASSEROLE

4 tablespoons butter
5 tablespoons flour
2 teaspoons curry powder
¼ teaspoon cumin
1 teaspoon salt
Dash freshly ground pepper
2½ cups chicken broth
2 tablespoons tomato paste
1 can (1 pound) whole onions, drained
3 cups cooked, diced potatoes

Heat butter in saucepan. Stir in flour and seasonings. Let bubble, then add broth. Cook and stir until mixture boils and thickens. Stir in tomato paste. Cut onions in half crosswise and mix with diced potatoes in a buttered 1½-quart casserole. Pour sauce over potato-onion mixture. Bake in a 375° F. oven 30 minutes. To make this casserole in advance, prepare potatoes, prepare sauce and refrigerate separately. At baking time, combine as directed. Add 15 minutes to baking time.

Makes 6 servings.

PRALINED YAMS

6 medium yams, cooked, peeled, and sliced (or 3 cans [1 pound each] yams, drained and sliced)
¼ cup melted butter
½ cup light corn syrup
3 tablespoons dark brown sugar
¼ cup chopped pecans

Place sliced yams in a buttered 1½-quart round casserole. Mix butter, syrup, sugar and pecans and pour over yams. Bake in 375° F. oven 30 to 40 minutes, basting frequently. This casserole can be prepared in advance, refrigerated and baked at serving time. Add 15 minutes to baking time.

Makes 6 servings.

YAMS WITH APPLES AND CURRANTS

4 medium yams, cooked, peeled, and sliced (or 2 cans
    [1 pound each] yams, drained)
¼ cup dark corn syrup
2 tablespoons dried currants*
2 tablespoons butter
1 tablespoon lemon juice
1 large tart apple, peeled and thinly sliced
2 tablespoons blanched almonds

Arrange yams in buttered shallow casserole. Combine remaining ingredients and cook over medium heat until apple slices are just tender. Pour over yams in casserole. Cover and bake in a 350° F. oven for 15 minutes or until bubbly. This casserole can be prepared in advance, refrigerated and baked at serving time. Add 15 minutes to cooking time.

Makes 4 servings.

* 2 tablespoons chopped raisins may be substituted

NEW ORLEANS YAMS

1 can (1 pound) grapefruit and orange sections
2 tablespoons honey
1 tablespoon cornstarch
¼ teaspoon salt
4 medium yams, cooked, peeled and halved lengthwise
    (or 2 cans [1 pound each] yams, drained)
Flaked coconut

Drain grapefruit and orange sections, reserving 1 cup syrup. Blend syrup with honey, cornstarch and salt in saucepan and cook and stir until mixture boils and is thickened. Arrange grapefruit and orange sections and yams in buttered shallow casserole and pour sauce over casserole. Sprinkle with coconut. Bake in a 375° F. oven for 15 minutes or until hot and bubbly. This casserole can be prepared in advance, refrigerated and baked at serving time. Add 15 minutes to baking time.

Makes 4 to 6 servings.

LOUISIANA YAM PECAN CASSEROLE

4 medium yams, cooked, peeled and mashed
1 tablespoon lemon juice
2 teaspoons grated lemon rind
½ cup chopped pecans
2 tablespoons butter
½ teaspoon salt
½ cup firmly packed brown sugar
2 tablespoons brown sugar
2 tablespoons chopped pecans
1 teaspoon grated lemon rind

Combine yams, lemon juice, 2 teaspoons lemon rind, ½ cup chopped pecans, butter, salt and ½ cup brown sugar. Mix well and spoon into a lightly buttered 1½-quart casserole. Combine remaining ingredients and sprinkle over yam mixture. Bake in 350° F. oven 20 minutes or until hot. This casserole can be prepared in advance, refrigerated and baked at serving time. Add 15 minutes to baking time.

Makes 4 servings.

SQUASH INCA

1 2-pound butternut squash
1 onion, sliced
½ teaspoon powdered cloves
½ teaspoon Tabasco
1 can (1 pound) tomatoes
3 tablespoons butter

Slice squash and remove peel, seeds and strings. Cook in boiling salted water until just tender (about 10 minutes). Alternate slices of onion with slices of squash in a buttered

2-quart casserole. Mix cloves and Tabasco with tomatoes and pour over squash. Dot top with butter. Bake in a 375° F. oven 30 minutes. This casserole can be prepared in advance, refrigerated and baked at serving time. Add 15 minutes to baking time.

Makes 6 servings.

BRIGHT BROCCOLI

1 package (10 ounces) frozen broccoli
1 can (1 pound) whole tomatoes
2 tablespoons butter
2 teaspoons flour
1 teaspoon minced onion
¼ teaspoon salt
¼ cup cracker crumbs
2 tablespoons grated Parmesan cheese

Cook broccoli according to package directions until almost tender. Drain. Drain tomatoes, reserve juice. Heat 1 tablespoon of butter with flour, onion and salt, then stir in tomato liquid. Cook and stir until mixture boils and is thickened. Place broccoli in center of buttered shallow 1-quart casserole. Slice tomatoes in half crosswise and arrange around broccoli. Spoon sauce over vegetables. Melt remaining tablespoon of butter and mix with crumbs and cheese. Sprinkle over casserole. Bake in a 350° F. oven for 20 minutes. This casserole can be prepared in advance, refrigerated, and baked at serving time. Add 15 minutes to baking time. Do not sprinkle crumb mixture on vegetables until casserole is ready to go into oven.

Makes 4 to 6 servings.

BRUSSELS SPROUTS EN CASSEROLE

1 quart fresh (or 2 packages [10 ounces] frozen) Brussels sprouts
1 cup boiling water
1½ teaspoons salt
1½ cups sliced celery
⅓ cup melted butter
3 tablespoons flour
¼ teaspoon freshly ground pepper
1⅓ cups milk
¾ cup dry breadcrumbs

Clean fresh Brussels sprouts and cook in boiling water with 1 teaspoon salt until just tender, about 15 minutes. Drain and save liquid. (Cook frozen Brussels sprouts in similar manner if used.) Sauté celery in 3 tablespoons butter for about 3 minutes. Sprinkle flour, remaining ½ teaspoon salt and pepper over celery and stir until bubbly. Gradually add milk and liquid from Brussels sprouts and cook and stir until mixture comes to a boil. Add cooked sprouts. Spoon mixture into a buttered 1½-quart casserole. Combine remaining butter with breadcrumbs. Sprinkle over sprouts and celery mixture in casserole. Bake in a 400° F. oven 15 to 20 minutes or until sprouts are heated through and crumbs are brown.

Makes 6 servings.

EGGPLANT TOMATO CASSEROLE

1 medium-sized eggplant
6 tomatoes
4 tablespoons butter
1 cup sliced fresh mushrooms
1 teaspoon salt
Dash freshly ground pepper
1 cup veal or beef stock

Peel eggplant and slice into thin slices. Peel tomatoes and slice into thin slices. Heat butter in skillet and sauté eggplant slices on both sides, then mushrooms until lightly browned. Season vegetables with salt and pepper. Arrange eggplant, tomatoes and mushrooms in alternate layers in a buttered 1½-quart casserole. Pour veal stock over vegetables. Cover. Bake in a 350° F. oven for 1 hour. This casserole can be prepared in advance, refrigerated and baked at serving time. Add 15 minutes to cooking time.

Makes 6 servings.

MOZZARELLA TOMATOES

1 package (6 ounces) mozarella cheese
1 can (1 pound) stewed tomatoes
3 slices toast, cubed
1 teaspoon onion powder
½ teaspoon salt
¼ teaspoon freshly ground pepper
¼ cup butter, melted

Reserve 4 strips of cheese for garnish. Cube remainder and combine with tomatoes and remaining ingredients. Pour into a buttered 1-quart casserole. Arrange reserved cheese strips on top. Bake in a 375° F. oven for 20 minutes or until bubbly. This casserole can be prepared in advance, refrigerated and baked at serving time. Add 10 minutes to baking time. Do not put strips of cheese on top until casserole is ready to go into the oven.

Makes 4 servings.

CASSEROLE CORN

1 cup soft breadcrumbs
2 tablespoons butter
1 can (12 ounces) whole kernel corn
2 eggs, beaten
1 can (10½ ounces) condensed cream-of-mushroom
     soup
¼ cup finely chopped onion
¼ teaspoon salt
⅛ teaspoon freshly ground pepper
¼ teaspoon celery salt

Cook breadcrumbs in butter until lightly browned. Mix with remaining ingredients and spoon into a buttered 1-quart casserole. Bake in a 350° F. oven about 40 minutes or until knife inserted into center comes out clean and mixture is firm. Serve at once.

Makes 6 servings.

CRISPY VEGETABLE CASSEROLE

3 cups cooked green beans
1 can (8 ounces) sliced water chestnuts, drained
1 can (4 ounces) sliced mushrooms, drained
1 can (10½ ounces) cream-of-mushroom soup
½ soup-can milk
1 cup chow-mein noodles

Mix green beans with water chestnuts and sliced mushrooms and spoon into a buttered 2-quart casserole. Combine soup with milk and pour over bean mixture. Sprinkle noodles over top. Bake in a 375° F. oven 15 to 20 minutes.

Makes 4 to 6 servings.

VEGETABLE SURPRISE

Cereal topping:
2 cups bite-size toasted corn cereal
¼ teaspoon salt
½ teaspoon onion powder
½ teaspoon ground basil
2 tablespoons melted butter
Vegetable mixture:
2 cans (16 ounces each) green beans, drained*
1 can (8 ounces) tomato sauce
½ teaspoon salt
⅛ teaspoon freshly ground pepper

Put corn cereal in bowl and crush to half its volume. Add salt, onion powder and basil and mix until thoroughly distributed. Drizzle butter over cereal and mix again.

Mix beans with tomato sauce and seasonings in a buttered 1½-quart casserole. Sprinkle cereal topping over vegetables. Bake in a 400° F. oven for 15 minutes or until thoroughly hot and topping browned.

Makes 6 servings.

* Lima beans, corn or peas may be substituted for green beans.

VEGETABLE CHEESE CASSEROLE

1 can (4 ounces) mushroom pieces and stems
2 cups sliced celery
1 package (9 ounces) frozen cut green beans
2 tablespoons finely chopped onion
4 tablespoons melted butter
2 tablespoons finely chopped celery leaves
1 can (10½ ounces) condensed Cheddar-cheese soup
1 can (10½ ounces) condensed cream-of-mushroom
   soup
½ teaspoon crushed dill weed
¼ teaspoon ground rosemary
⅛ teaspoon white pepper
4 cups bite-size toasted corn cereal

Drain mushroom liquid into saucepan. Add celery and green beans. Cover and cook 10 minutes or until almost tender. Drain. Cook onion in 2 tablespoons of the butter until soft but not browned. Add mushrooms and celery leaves and cook until mushrooms are lightly browned. Combine beans and celery with mushroom mixture, soups, dill, rosemary and pepper. Spoon into buttered 2-quart casserole. Crush corn cereal and mix with remaining 2 tablespoons butter and sprinkle over vegetable mixture. Bake in 350° F. oven 20 minutes or until brown and bubbling. This casserole can be prepared in advance, refrigerated and baked at serving time. Add 15 minutes to baking time. Put cereal crumbs on top just before casserole goes into oven.

Makes 8 servings.

RICE SOUR-CREAM PILAF

1 can (4 ounces) sliced mushrooms
Chicken broth
1⅓ cups precooked rice
2 tablespoons butter
½ cup dairy sour cream

Drain liquid from mushrooms. Measure and add chicken broth to make 2¼ cups. Combine with mushrooms, rice and butter in a buttered 1-quart casserole. Cover and bake in a 375° F. oven for 20 minutes or until rice is tender. Remove from oven, stir in sour cream and serve.

Makes 4 servings.

HOLIDAY RICE

1½ cups chicken broth
⅛ teaspoon poultry seasoning
Salt to taste
2 tablespoons butter
½ tablespoon chopped onion
1⅓ cups precooked rice
¼ cup chopped parsley
¼ cup coarsely chopped pistachio nuts

Combine chicken broth with remaining ingredients in a buttered 3-cup casserole. Cover and bake in a 375° F. oven for 20 minutes or until rice is tender.

Makes 4 servings.

YORKVILLE MACARONI

½ pound sliced bacon
1 large onion, sliced
½ pound elbow macaroni, cooked and drained
1 cup (8-ounce can) tomato sauce
2 cups canned apple sauce
1 cup shredded natural sharp cheese
⅛ teaspoon dry mustard
½ teaspoon Worcestershire sauce
½ teaspoon salt
¼ teaspoon freshly ground pepper

Fry bacon until crisp, drain on paper towels. Reserve 4 or 5 slices for garnish, crumble remaining slices. Sauté onion slices in a little of the bacon drippings. Combine all ingredients, stirring in crumbled bacon. Place mixture into a 2-quart buttered casserole and bake in a 350° F. oven for 25 minutes. About 5 minutes before baking is completed, arrange reserved bacon slices on top of casserole mixture.

Makes 4 to 6 servings.

CORN SPOON BREAD

½ cup all-purpose flour
2 teaspoons baking powder
2 tablespoons sugar
1 teaspoon salt
¾ cup yellow cornmeal
1 egg, beaten
1 cup canned cream-style corn
¾ cup milk
4 tablespoons butter, melted

Sift flour with baking powder, sugar and salt. Mix in cornmeal. Combine egg with corn, milk and butter. Add to flour mixture, stirring just to blend. Pour into buttered 1-quart casserole. Bake in a 400° F. oven for 45 minutes.

Makes 6 servings.

SPOON BREAD

½ cup boiling water
1 cup cornmeal
3 eggs
2 tablespoons butter, melted
2 teaspoons baking powder
½ teaspoon salt
1 cup milk

In a bowl, mix boiling water with cornmeal. Stir until smooth and cool. Beat in eggs one at a time, beating well after each addition. Add remaining ingredients, mixing well. Pour in a buttered 1-quart casserole. Bake in a 350° F. oven for about 45 minutes or until browned. Serve at once with butter.

Makes 4 to 6 servings.

MISS INA'S SHERRIED BANANAS

8 medium-ripe bananas
¼ pound (½ cup) butter
1 cup sugar
⅔ cup dry sack sherry

Peel bananas and sauté in butter until lightly browned on all sides. Add sugar and then sherry to bananas in skillet and cook until liquid bubbles and sugar is melted. Transfer bananas to buttered shallow casserole. Pour sherry sauce over. Cover and bake in a 375° F. oven for about 20 minutes or until sherry sauce bubbles.

Makes 8 servings.

QUICK 'N' EASY CASSEROLES

All of us need a few quick 'n' easy recipes to pull out of the hat when the occasion arises, and this section is devoted to that purpose. Some of the recipes are planned so that the ingredients can be stored on the pantry shelf, ready when an emergency arises. Others need some food items that are better purchased as used. But all the recipes take a minimum of work to produce a maximum of savory flavor.

TURKEY SUPPER

1¾ cups fresh green beans, cut (or 1 package [10 ounces] frozen cut green beans)
1¼ cups boiling water
2½ cups cooked, diced turkey
1 can (10½ ounces) condensed cream-of-mushroom soup
¼ teaspoon salt
⅛ teaspoon freshly ground pepper
1 cup packaged precooked rice
1 can (3½ ounces) French-fried onion rings
6 tomato slices

Cook green beans in boiling water 5 minutes. Add turkey, soup and seasonings to green beans and cook 2 minutes longer. Stir in rice and half the onion rings. Pour into buttered

251

2-quart casserole. Arrange remaining onion rings and tomato slices on top. Bake in a 400° F. oven 20 to 25 minutes.

Makes 4 to 6 servings.

CHICKEN NEWBURG CASSEROLE

3 tablespoons chopped onion
1 tablespoon butter
1 can (10½ ounces) cream-of-chicken soup
½ cup milk
2 cups diced cooked chicken
1 egg, beaten
2 tablespoons sherry
½ cup shredded sharp Cheddar cheese

Cook onion in butter until tender but not browned. Mix with soup, milk, chicken, egg and sherry. Spoon into 2 buttered individual casseroles or a 1-quart casserole and sprinkle grated cheese on top. Bake in a 400° F. oven 20 minutes for individuals, 30 minutes for large dish, or until mixture is bubbly and cheese melted.

Makes 2 servings.

BAKED CHICKEN CURRY

2 cans (5 to 6 ounces each) boned chicken
1 can (10½ ounces) condensed cream-of-chicken soup
⅓ cup undiluted evaporated milk
2 teaspoons curry powder
¼ teaspoon ginger
¼ teaspoon liquid garlic
1 cup cooked peas, drained

Cut chicken into large dice and mix lightly with remaining ingredients. Spoon into buttered shallow 1½-quart casserole. Bake in a 400° F. oven for about 20 minutes or until mixture is bubbly and hot.

Makes 4 servings.

CHICKEN SUPREME

4 tablespoons flour
2½ cups chicken broth
1¼ cups shredded sharp Cheddar cheese
5 cups diced cooked chicken
Salt and freshly ground pepper to taste
1 can (8 ounces) artichoke hearts, drained
1 can (1 pound) asparagus spears, drained

Blend flour with ½ cup of the broth in a saucepan. Gradually stir in remaining broth. Place over medium heat and cook and stir until mixture boils and is thickened. Add 1 cup cheese and stir until melted. Remove from heat and stir in chicken. Season to taste with salt and pepper. Alternate layers of chicken mixture with vegetables in a 3-quart casserole. Sprinkle remaining cheese on top. Bake in a 375° F. oven for 15 to 20 minutes.

Makes 6 servings.

PENTHOUSE CASSEROLE

1 package (14 ounces) deluxe-type macaroni and cheese
    dinner
1 can (10½ ounces) condensed cream-of-celery soup
1 can (7 ounces) crabmeat, drained, flaked
½ cup milk
1 can (3 ounces) sliced mushrooms
1 teaspoon instant minced onion
1 cup fresh breadcrumbs
¼ cup melted butter

Prepare dinner as directed on package. Add soup, crab-meat, milk, mushrooms and liquid, and onion. Mix well and spoon into a 2-quart casserole. Toss breadcrumbs with melted butter and sprinkle on top of macaroni mixture. Bake in a 350° F. oven for 30 minutes or until hot and bubbly.

Makes 6 servings.

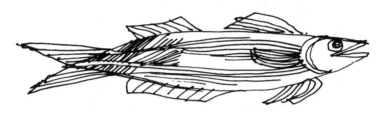

TEXAS TUNA

2 cans (7 ounces each) tuna
2 cans (1 pound each) kidney beans, drained
1 can (1 pound 4 ounces) whole tomatoes
1 tablespoon instant minced onion
2 teaspoons chili powder
½ teaspoon salt
¼ teaspoon Tabasco
¼ teaspoon oregano
½ cup cornflake crumbs

In a 3-quart casserole, combine tuna, kidney beans and tomatoes with onion, chili powder, salt, Tabasco, oregano and ¼ cup cornflake crumbs. Mix lightly to blend ingredients. Sprinkle remaining cornflake crumbs on top. Bake in a 425° F. oven for about 25 minutes or until heated through. This casserole can be prepared in advance, refrigerated and heated when ready to serve. Add 15 minutes to cooking time.

Makes 6 servings.

TUNA AND GREEN BEANS PRONTO

1 can (7 ounces) tuna, drained
1 cup canned green beans, drained
¼ cup blue-cheese dressing
½ cup dairy sour cream
1 tablespoon melted butter
1 cup soft breadcrumbs

Flake drained tuna in small bowl. Gently mix in green beans. Combine blue-cheese dressing with sour cream. Alternate two layers each of tuna and sour-cream mixtures in a 3-cup casserole. Mix just enough to allow sour cream to seep to bottom of casserole. Top with breadcrumbs mixed with butter. Bake in a 350° F. oven for 15 to 20 minutes.

Makes 2 servings.

CASSEROLE À LA NAPLES

1 can (10½ ounces) condensed mushroom soup
1 cup dry white wine
½ cup water
1 teaspoon MSG
2 teaspoons instant minced onion
1 teaspoon dill weed
¼ teaspoon Tabasco
1½ cups packaged precooked rice
1 can (5 ounces) shrimp, drained
1 can (4 ounces) pimiento, drained, cut into large dice
1 can (7 ounces) lobster, drained
1 can (6½ ounces) crab, drained, cartilage removed
¼ cup chopped parsley

Combine soup with wine, water, seasonings, and rice in a 2½-quart casserole. Reserve several shrimp and about half of diced pimiento for top of casserole. Add remaining shrimp, pimiento, lobster and crab to mixture in casserole. Arrange reserved shrimp and pimiento on top. Cover and bake in a 350° F. oven for 30 minutes. Garnish with chopped parsley.

Makes 6 servings.

TUNA MONTE CRISTO

½ cup chopped green pepper
¼ cup chopped onion
3 tablespoons butter
2 cans (7 ounces each) tuna, drained
½ cup mayonnaise
½ teaspoon salt
2 cups dairy sour cream
1 package (8 ounces) frozen pancakes, defrosted
¼ cup light cream
½ cup shredded Cheddar cheese

Cook green pepper and onion in butter until tender. Mix with tuna, mayonnaise, salt and 1 cup sour cream. Line bottom of buttered 2-quart casserole with half the pancakes. Spoon on tuna mixture. Top with remaining pancakes. Mix 1 cup sour cream and cream and spread over pancakes. Sprinkle with cheese. Bake in a 350° F. oven for 30 minutes or until heated through.

Makes 4 servings.

ONION CHEESE STRATA

8 slices bread
8 slices (1 ounce each) processed American cheese
3 to 4 cups thin onion rings
2 eggs
2 cups milk
1 tablespoon prepared mustard
1 teaspoon salt
1 teaspoon paprika

Trim crusts from bread. Place 4 slices in the bottom of a square 9-inch casserole. Place 4 cheese slices over bread and then sprinkle on half the onion slices. Repeat. Beat eggs with milk, mustard and salt. Mix well and pour over mixture in baking dish. Sprinkle with paprika. Bake in a 350° F. oven about 45 minutes or until browned.

Makes 4 servings.

NEW BEDFORD POTATO PIE

½ cup sliced celery
2 tablespoons chopped onion
2 tablespoons butter
1 can (10 ounces) frozen condensed cream-of-shrimp
    soup, defrosted
½ cup milk
1 can (6 ounces) shrimp, drained
1 can (6 ounces) lobster, drained
½ cup cooked peas
Dash Angostura bitters
Dash ground thyme
1 cup mashed potatoes (or ¼ cup instant mashed
    potato, prepared as directed on package)
2 tablespoons shredded sharp cheese

Cook celery and onion in butter until tender. Blend in soup, milk, shrimp, lobster, peas, bitters and thyme. Heat slowly, stirring. Pour into a 1½-quart buttered casserole. Arrange potatoes around edge of casserole. Sprinkle with cheese. Bake in a 450° F. oven 15 minutes or until potatoes are browned. This casserole can be prepared in advance. Refrigerate and add the potato border just before baking. Increase baking time 15 minutes.

Makes 4 servings.

BAKED BEAN FRANKFURTER CASSEROLE

¼ cup unsulphured molasses
1 tablespoon vinegar
1 tablespoon prepared mustard
3 cans (1 pound each) baked beans in tomato sauce
1 medium onion, sliced
16 frankfurters

Combine molasses, vinegar and mustard and mix well. Empty beans into a flat 2-quart casserole and stir in molasses mixture. Arrange onion slices and frankfurters on top of beans. Bake in a 375° F. oven 35 minutes. This casserole can be prepared in advance, refrigerated, and baked at serving time. Add 15 minutes to baking time.

Makes 6 to 8 servings.

HASH ANDOVER

1 can (15½ ounces) corned-beef hash
¼ cup cocktail onions, drained and chopped
¼ cup chili sauce
1 can (7 ounces) whole kernel corn, drained
1 slice bacon, diced

Mix hash with onions and chili sauce. Spoon around the outside edge of a buttered 1-quart casserole. Fill center with corn. Bake in a 400° F. oven for 30 minutes.

Makes 2 servings.

MOD FRANK CASSEROLE

2 tablespoons salad oil
½ cup chopped onion
2 cans (12 ounces each) frankfurters
2 cans (1 pound each) pork and beans
1¾ cups canned apple sauce
2 tablespoons prepared mustard
¼ cup chili sauce
3 thin slices American cheese

Heat oil in skillet and cook onion for 3 minutes or until tender but not browned. Cut frankfurters in ½-inch pieces and add to onion in skillet. Brown lightly. Spoon into a 3-quart casserole. Add pork and beans, apple sauce, mustard and chili sauce and stir to blend. Bake in a 350° F. oven for 30 minutes. Arrange cheese on top in a decorative pattern. Bake several minutes longer or until cheese has melted.

Makes 6 servings.

CASSEROLE DESSERTS

Desserts baked in casseroles are generally quite filling. Recipes such as raisin-rice pudding, date-bread pudding, or Indian pudding are a heritage from the days when a hearty dessert followed a meal of similar proportions. Today we can serve these marvelous old-timers when the meal itself is a lightweight.

But the dessert soufflé is an exception. It is one of the famous glamour-girl desserts along with the Crêpes Suzette (p. 120) and the Cherries Jubilee (p. 118). Two of the secrets of soufflé are well-beaten egg yolks and stiffly beaten egg whites. Timing is all-important. Better the guests wait for the soufflé than the soufflé for the guests. The latter is disastrous.

Along with the hearty old-timers and the glamorous dessert soufflés are fruit desserts, which will also help you to use your casserole for a double-duty dish.

POT DE CRÈME CHOCOLAT

2 cups light cream
Dash salt
¼ cup sugar
1 package (4 ounces) sweet cooking-chocolate
1 teaspoon vanilla
6 egg yolks
Whipped cream

Scald cream with salt, sugar and chocolate over low heat, stirring until chocolate is melted and blended with cream. Cool slightly. Add vanilla. Beat egg yolks until thick and lemon-colored. Stir in chocolate mixture. Strain into a 1-quart casserole and set in a pan of hot water. Bake in a 350° F. oven for 30 minutes or until a knife inserted in center comes out clean. Chill. Serve with whipped cream.

Makes 4 to 6 servings.

CHOCOLATE MINT CREAM

2 squares (1 ounce each) unsweetened chocolate
1 cup light cream
1 cup soft breadcrumbs
3 tablespoons white crème de menthe
½ cup sugar
¼ teaspoon salt
1 tablespoon butter
3 eggs, separated
Whipped cream

Melt chocolate and cream over low heat, stirring until blended. Mix in crumbs, crème de menthe, sugar, salt and butter. Beat egg yolks slightly and fold into chocolate mixture. Cool. Beat egg whites until stiff and fold into cooled mixture. Pour into a buttered 1-quart casserole and bake in a 350° F. oven for 35 to 40 minutes. Serve hot or cold with whipped cream.

Makes 4 to 6 servings.

SOUFFLÉ AU LIQUEUR

¼ cup flour
½ cup sugar
¼ teaspoon salt
1 cup light cream
2 tablespoons butter
4 tablespoons Cointreau, curaçao, crème de cacao, or
    other favorite liqueur
4 eggs, separated
¼ cup finely chopped mixed candied fruits soaked in
    2 tablespoons same liqueur as used above
2 cups strawberries mixed with ½ cup liqueur used
    above

Mix flour, sugar and salt in saucepan. Slowly stir in cream. Cook and stir over medium heat until mixture boils and is thickened. Stir in butter and liqueur. Beat egg whites until very stiff. Beat egg yolks until thick and lemon-colored. Fold into sauce mixture. Fold into egg whites and candied fruits. Pour into 1½-quart casserole. Bake in a 425° F. oven for 25 minutes or until well browned, using lower shelf of oven. Serve at once from the casserole with strawberries soaked in liqueur.

Makes 4 to 6 servings.

ORANGE SOUFFLÉ

3 eggs, separated
½ cup sugar
3 tablespoons flour
2 tablespoons melted butter
½ cup evaporated milk
1 tablespoon grated orange rind
1 cup orange juice (fresh or reconstituted frozen)
¼ teaspoon salt

Beat egg yolks with 2 tablespoons of the sugar. Stir in flour and melted butter. Gradually add evaporated milk, orange rind and orange juice. Blend until smooth. Beat egg whites and salt until stiff but not dry. Gradually add remaining sugar and beat until very stiff. Fold in egg-yolk mixture. Pour into unbuttered 2-quart casserole. Place in a pan of boiling water that comes to half the depth of the casserole. Bake in a 325° F. oven for 35 to 40 minutes or until knife can be inserted and comes out clean. Serve immediately.

Makes 6 servings.

Note: If an emergency arises and the soufflé can't be served IMMEDIATELY, turn oven heat to lowest heat to hold soufflé.

VANILLA SOUFFLÉ

¼ cup flour
½ cup sugar
¼ teaspoon salt
1 cup milk
2 tablespoons butter
4 eggs, separated
1 teaspoon vanilla

Mix flour, sugar and salt in saucepan. Slowly stir in milk. Cook and stir over medium heat until mixture boils and is thickened. Stir in butter. Beat egg whites until very stiff. Beat egg yolks until thick and lemon-colored. Fold in sauce mixture. Fold into egg whites and vanilla. Pour into 1½-quart casserole. Bake in a 425° F. oven for 25 minutes or until well browned, using lower shelf of oven. Serve at once from the casserole. Serve with fruit sauce if desired.

Makes 4 to 6 servings.

VARIATION:

Chocolate Soufflé: Stir 2 squares melted unsweetened chocolate into cooked milk mixture before adding to egg yolks.

SHERRIED LEMON PUDDING

3 tablespoons butter
⅔ cup sugar
2 eggs, separated
3 tablespoons lemon juice
¼ cup sweet sherry
1 teaspoon grated lemon rind
3 tablespoons flour
1 cup milk

Cream butter with sugar until light and fluffy. Beat egg yolk until thick and lemon-colored. Add to creamed mixture. Stir in lemon juice, sherry and rind. Add flour and milk. Beat egg whites until stiff and fold into first mixture. Pour into buttered 1½-quart casserole and set in a pan of hot water up to the level of the pudding. Bake in a 375° F. oven 35 to 40 minutes. Cool. Serve plain or with whipped cream.
Makes 4 to 6 servings.

APPLE SPOON PUDDING

1 cup sugar
1 cup all-purpose flour, sifted
1 teaspoon soda
1 teaspoon cinnamon
¼ teaspoon cloves
¼ cup melted butter
1 egg, well beaten
2½ cups chopped tart apple
1 pint vanilla ice cream

Sift together sugar, flour, soda and spices into a bowl. Add remaining ingredients, stirring to blend and form a soft dough. Spoon into buttered 1½-quart casserole. Bake in a 350° F. oven 35 minutes. Serve hot, topped with a spoon of vanilla ice cream.

Makes 6 servings.

APPLE RUM MERINGUE PUDDING

2 cups canned apple sauce
1 cup light brown sugar
1 cup broken pecans
1 cup raisins
¼ cup rum
2 teaspoons cinnamon
1 teaspoon nutmeg
½ teaspoon allspice
4 egg whites
1 teaspoon lemon extract
½ cup sugar

Mix apple sauce, brown sugar, pecans, raisins, rum and spices and heat. Pour into a 1½-quart casserole. Beat egg whites stiff and fold in lemon extract. Gradually beat in ½ cup sugar until mixture stands in stiff peaks. Spread over top of apple-sauce mixture in casserole. Bake in a 325° F. oven for 15 to 20 minutes or until meringue is delicately browned. Serve at once.

Makes 6 servings.

APPLE-SPICE SWIRLS

1 cup apple juice
1 cup granulated sugar
2 tablespoons lemon juice
1½ cups all-purpose flour
1 teaspoon salt
3 teaspoons baking powder
½ cup butter
½ cup rolled oats
½ cup milk
1 tablespoon melted butter
1½ cups canned apple sauce
½ cup brown sugar
1 teaspoon cinnamon
½ teaspoon nutmeg
1 teaspoon grated lemon rind
½ cup chopped walnuts

To make syrup: combine apple juice, granulated sugar and lemon juice. Simmer for 10 minutes; reserve. To make pastry: combine flour, salt and baking powder. Cut in ½ cup butter until mixture resembles coarse crumbs. Add oats and milk, mixing lightly until mixture clears the bowl. Roll out to a 13x9-inch rectangle. Brush with the tablespoon of melted butter. Mix together remaining ingredients. Spread apple-sauce mixture on dough and roll up loosely, as for jelly roll, sealing edges. (Roll loosely to accommodate all of the filling.) Cut into 9 slices, each about 1 inch wide. Place slices in round 8-inch casserole. Pour reserved syrup over top and bake in a 400° F. oven 35 minutes. Serve warm, with cream if desired.

Makes 6 to 8 servings.

PERSIAN APPLES

1 cup pitted dates
4 large tart apples
½ cup granulated sugar
½ cup chopped pecans
¾ cup flour
½ teaspoon salt
½ cup brown sugar
1 teaspoon cinnamon
½ cup butter

Cut dates crosswise. Peel and slice apples. Combine apples and dates with ½ cup granulated sugar and chopped pecans and put into a buttered 1½-quart casserole. Mix flour, salt, brown sugar and cinnamon together. Cut in butter until mixture is consistency of cornmeal. Spoon over apples and dates in casserole. Bake in a 375° F. oven for 35 minutes or until apples are tender.

Makes 4 to 6 servings.

APPLE BROWN BETTY

4 cups soft breadcrumbs
½ cup melted butter
3 cups canned apple sauce
⅓ cup brown sugar
2 tablespoons lemon juice
½ teaspoon lemon rind, grated
1 teaspoon cinnamon
¼ teaspoon ground nutmeg
Cream

Mix breadcrumbs with butter in skillet. Cook and stir over low heat until crumbs are lightly browned. Pour half of the crumbs into a shallow 1½-quart casserole. Spread evenly over bottom. Mix apple sauce with sugar, lemon juice and rind and spices. Spoon over crumbs in casserole. Top with remaining crumbs. Bake in a 350° F. oven for 30 minutes or until top is well browned. Serve warm with cream.

Makes 6 servings.

BAKED PEARS EN CASSEROLE

6 pears
½ cup chopped seedless raisins
¼ cup brown sugar
1 teaspoon grated lemon rind
¾ cup Sauterne wine
¼ cup brandy
½ cup macaroon crumbs

Peel and core pears and slice into thin slices. Mix raisins, sugar and lemon rind and arrange alternately with pear slices in a buttered 1-quart casserole. Pour wine and brandy over pears. Cover and bake in a 350° F. oven for 30 minutes. Uncover, sprinkle macaroon crumbs on top and bake another 10 minutes or until crumbs are browned.

Makes 4 to 6 servings.

BRANDIED PEACH PUDDING

⅓ cup butter, softened
½ cup sugar
3 eggs, separated
3 tablespoons brandy
1 cup dry macaroon crumbs
1 cup finely chopped fresh or frozen peaches
¼ teaspoon salt

Cream butter with sugar until light and fluffy. Add egg yolks one at a time, beating after each addition. Stir in brandy, macaroon crumbs and peaches. Beat egg whites with salt until stiff. Fold into peach mixture. Pour into a buttered 1½-quart casserole. Bake in a 325° F. oven 30 to 40 minutes or until browned. Serve at once.

Makes 4 to 6 servings.

BANANAS DEL MAR

6 bananas
½ cup orange juice
¼ cup Curacao
¼ cup sugar
2 tablespoons butter
¾ cup flaked coconut

Peel bananas and cut in half lengthwise. Arrange in a well-buttered flat casserole. Mix orange juice with Curacao and sugar. Pour over bananas. Dot with butter. Sprinkle coconut over mixture. Bake in a 400° F. oven about 15 minutes or until the coconut is lightly browned. Serve with dairy sour cream if desired.

Makes 6 servings.

BANANAS TAHITI

4 ripe bananas
½ cup apricot jam
½ cup sweet sherry
¼ cup melted butter
¼ cup lemon juice
¼ cup brown sugar

Peel and cut bananas in half lengthwise. Arrange in a buttered shallow casserole and spread with jam. Mix sherry with remaining ingredients. Spoon over bananas in dish. Bake in a 350° F. oven for 20 to 25 minutes. Baste bananas with sauce several times during baking. Serve warm with sauce from casserole.

Makes 4 servings.

FRUIT CURRY

2 cans (1 pound each) fruits for salad
¼ cup light brown sugar
2 teaspoons curry powder
2 tablespoons butter
½ cup dairy sour cream

Drain fruit. Arrange in a 1-quart casserole. Mix brown sugar and curry powder together and sprinkle over fruit. Dot top with butter. Bake in a 350° F. oven for 20 minutes. Serve hot with a spoon of sour cream. This casserole can be prepared in advance and baked when ready to serve. If the variation with the corn-flake topping is to be used, add that just before casserole goes in to bake.

Makes 4 to 6 servings.

VARIATION:

Combine 1 cup corn flakes, slightly crushed, with 2 tablespoons brown sugar and 2 tablespoons melted butter and sprinkle over fruit and curry mixture. Bake as directed. Serve warm with or without sour cream.

CHÂTEAU FRUIT CASSEROLE

1 can (1 pound 13 ounces) pear halves, well drained
1 can (1 pound 13 ounces) sliced peaches, well drained
1 cup fresh blueberries or 1 can (8 ounces) purple plums, well drained
1½ cups dairy sour cream
1 teaspoon vanilla extract
2 eggs, slightly beaten
⅓ cup light brown sugar, firmly packed
3 tablespoons flour
2 tablespoons soft butter
1 tablespoon grated lemon rind
¼ teaspoon grated nutmeg
20 shortbread cookies, crumbled

Arrange fruit in a buttered 1½-quart casserole. Stir sour cream and vanilla into eggs. Mix together 3 tablespoons sugar and 1 tablespoon flour. Add to sour-cream mixture. Pour over fruits. Bake in a 350° F. oven 15 minutes. While fruit bakes, blend butter with remainder of sugar and flour, then add lemon rind, nutmeg and shortbread cookies. Mix lightly. Sprinkle over fruit. Bake 10 to 15 minutes longer. Let stand 5 minutes before serving.

Makes 8 servings.

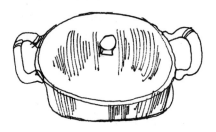

FROZEN FRUIT COBBLER

2 packages (12 ounces each) frozen mixed fruit
2 tablespoons cornstarch
2 tablespoons sugar
¼ teaspoon cinnamon
2 tablespoons butter
2 cups biscuit mix
2 tablespoons sugar
⅔ cup milk

Defrost fruit and pour into buttered 1-quart casserole. Mix in cornstarch, 2 tablespoons sugar and cinnamon. Dot with butter. Combine biscuit mix with 2 tablespoons sugar and milk. Pat out to ¼-inch thickness in shape to fit casserole and put on top of fruit. Bake in a 500° F. oven about 40 minutes. Serve warm with whipped topping, softened vanilla ice cream or cream.

Makes 6 servings.

BAKED RICE RAISIN PUDDING

4 cups milk
¼ cup rice
½ cup sugar
¼ teaspoon nutmeg
1 teaspoon vanilla
1 tablespoon butter
½ cup raisins

Scald milk and mix with remaining ingredients. Pour into a buttered 1½-quart casserole. Bake in a 325° F. oven about 2½ hours. Stir occasionally, but do not stir during the last half-hour of baking. Serve warm plain or with cream.

Makes 6 servings.

CAKE RAISIN PUDDING

2 cups milk
½ cup raisins
2 tablespoons sugar
3 tablespoons butter
2 cups cake crumbs
2 eggs, beaten
¼ teaspoon salt
1 teaspoon vanilla

Scald milk and raisins together. Add sugar and butter and cool. Stir in remaining ingredients and pour into buttered 1-quart casserole. Set in a pan of hot water up to the level of the pudding. Bake in a 375° F. oven about 1 hour.

Makes 4 to 6 servings.

VARIATION:

> Substitute 1 cup grapenuts cereal for the cake crumbs.
> Heat grapenuts with milk and raisins.

ORANGE CARAMEL PUDDING

1¼ cups sugar
2 tablespoons butter
1 teaspoon salt
¼ teaspoon grated orange rind
6 eggs, separated
¼ cup flour
1¼ cups orange juice (fresh or reconstituted frozen)
Sliced orange and whipped cream if desired

Melt ½ cup of the sugar in small skillet over low heat until light brown syrup is formed, stirring constantly. Pour into
bottom of a 1½-quart casserole. Cream butter with remain-

ing ¾ cup sugar until light. Add salt and rind. Add egg yolks, one at a time, beating well after each addition. Add flour and mix well. Stir in orange juice. Beat egg whites until very stiff. Fold orange mixture into egg whites. Pour over syrup in casserole. Place in pan of hot water that comes to half the depth of the casserole. Bake in a 350° F. oven for about an hour or until the top is firm when touched with the finger. Cool and chill. If desired, garnish the pudding with orange slices and whipped cream when ready to serve.

Makes 6 servings.

BAKED INDIAN PUDDING

1 cup yellow cornmeal
½ cup dark molasses
¼ cup granulated sugar
¼ cup butter
¼ teaspoon salt
¼ teaspoon baking soda
2 eggs, beaten
1½ quarts hot milk
1 pint vanilla ice cream

Mix all ingredients thoroughly with half the hot milk. Spoon into a buttered 2-quart ceramic casserole and bake in a 450° F. oven until mixture boils (about 30 minutes). Stir in remaining milk. Reduce heat to 300° F. and bake for 5 hours, stirring occasionally. Serve hot, topped with a spoon of vanilla ice cream.

Makes 4 servings.

INDEX